playing live

THE COMPLETE GUIDE TO

playing live

Paul Charles

OMNIBUS PRESS

London/New York/Paris/Sydney/Copenhagen/Madrid/Tokyo

Cover designed by Chloë Alexander

ISBN: 0.7119.9835.3
Order No: OP 49445

Exclusive Distributors:
Music Sales Limited,
8/9 Frith Street,
London W1D 3JB, UK.

Music Sales Corporation,
257 Park Avenue South,
New York, NY 10010, USA.

Macmillan Distribution Services,
53 Park West Drive,
Derrimut, Vic 3030,
Australia.

To the Music Trade only:
Music Sales Limited,
8/9 Frith Street,
London W1D 3JB, UK.

Typeset by Galleon Typesetting, Ipswich
Printed in Great Britain by Creative Print & Design, Wales

A catalogue record for this book is available from
the British Library.

www.omnibuspress.com

CONTENTS

INTRODUCTION

The first live music I can remember ever hearing was in a wee Village Hall in Rasharkin in Northern Ireland. The band playing was called The Driftwoods and they did an ace version of 'She Thinks I Still Care', which in its original format, 'He Thinks I Still Care', had been a hit for Connie Francis.

I remember it being a very exciting night, probably because I was entering a new world and was experiencing that unforgettable buzz for the first time. You had the mixture of my nervousness of this new and colourful adult environment, of experiencing real live musicians, seeing people up on a stage – literally about three feet away – who could actually perform and sing the songs I'd been enjoying on the wireless for the previous few years. There were amplifiers with regal rows of controls and there was an echo unit with red lights and green magic eyes, which moved with the music, confirming, I suppose, that the music performed on stage really was live. There were microphones, which looked like shrunken skulls; masculine, yet elegant; guitars; a ragtag and bobtail drum kit and a shiny golden saxophone. And all were being professionally used and mastered, unlike the static catalogue shots I'd been looking at with envy over the previous months. Of course there were the musicians, but there were certainly no lawyers, managers, accountants, agents, roadies, sound engineers or lighting designers. No, all of that was to come later. On that first night there were just four musicians swapping positions and instruments, *playing live* and making music.

There were girls, too, and the whole ritual – three dance sets; ladies' choice; lemonade breaks; chatting up, and, most importantly, blagging the last dance – all of which I learned pretty quickly. So quickly I even managed to walk Maureen home. Maureen was one of the prettiest girls (at least through my spectacles) in the hall. I suppose that's another reason the night burned its way permanently into my memory cells.

I'm not about to say that that particular night changed my life. Hey, and you know what, maybe it did. But it was the start, my beginning in a lifelong fascination and involvement with live music.

A few years, and many dances later, some schoolmates and myself formed a group called Goggles Anonymous for a school variety show. The name? Okay, we all wore glasses and Hedgehoppers Anonymous were enjoying their first success at the time. For some strange reason, one I've never been able to work out – might have had something to do with the fact that I was the only one who had the record – but I routined the group through the harmonies of The Beach Boys' 'Sloop John B'. Talk about the completely blind leading the near blind. I don't have an ounce of music in my body, never had. I think it's fair to say at this stage in my life that I never will. I can't play an instrument and I couldn't sing to save my life, so the performance must have been pretty bizarre. I do remember a few of the wee girls screaming with excitement like they did on the telly. Perhaps what I was hearing, from my vantage point at the back of the hall, were cries of agony. Suffice to say the Goggles Anonymous debut was also their swan song.

Then wouldn't you know it but didn't one of my mates in Goggles Anonymous go and form a wee group called Blues By Five – there were five of them and they played the blues, right – and, as my next-door neighbour, Dixie Kerr, played saxophone in a local showband, The Breakaways, I was given the task of asking Dixie if the Blues By Five could play relief to The Breakaways. Okay, time out. As I go through this, I keep coming across things that I feel a need to explain, so I hope you'll forgive me the slight detours. Don't worry, I will keep returning to the main road. Relief groups, yes they were what distracted me. Right. The showbands were the BIG thing in Ireland from the mid-Fifties to the late Sixties. Showbands, such as The Royal, The Dixies and The Freshmen were like travelling live jukeboxes covering UK and US hits in the numerous Irish ballrooms. Originally they played from 8.00 pm to 2.00 am, then they started realising that the dancers were happy to spend the first three and a half hours in the local pubs, so, rather than playing to empty ballrooms, they employed relief groups to play to the empty ballrooms so they could enjoy the craic in the pubs themselves.

I managed to secure a few relief spots for the Blues By Five with The Breakaways, and by default, I became *the* manager. The manager's role was basically someone who didn't play music but who had mates who did, and so the manager helped do all the stuff that needed doing to get *the boys* up on stage. Being the manager meant a lot of blagging and basically that's what I've been doing ever since.

The job description has changed somewhat, mainly because there are now managers, lawyers, accountants, sound engineers, lighting designers, stage technicians (roadies), merchandisers, bus drivers, truck drivers, choreographers, image consultants, promoters, publicists, radio pluggers, travel agents, ambience directors (drug dealers), fitness instructors, security personnel and, my particular career choice, agents all helping to put *the boys* and/or girls up on stage every night.

★

Even today, after having done this professionally for 25 years, I still get asked, "Yes, but what do you actually *do* as an agent?"

So, I suppose explaining that as well as explaining what is involved in Playing Live, is really what *Playing Live* (the book) is all about. It's about getting started; what would-be artists need; what the back-up team do; what they'll charge; how to find them; how to make money; and how to keep doing it. I'll also discuss all the potential by-products of Playing Live (as a career), everything from radio, television, songwriting, making records, merchandising, sponsorship, acting and even the dubious business of politics.

On top of which, since you've invested in the price of this book, we'll signpost all of the above with some tales of glory and woe from those who have gone before you.

I can't guarantee it'll turn you into the biggest rock star of the 21st century but at the very least it'll explain the mechanics of how today's big rock stars ended up where they are, offer a road map of how to get there and, if you absorb it all correctly, help you avoid getting stiffed.

Paul Charles, September 2003

1

A BRIEF HISTORY

Following the Second World War, the youth of the United Kingdom of Great Britain and Northern Ireland found themselves developing a very excusable live-and-play-for-today attitude. Add to that the fact that they had more change in their pockets and more time on their hands than the pre-war generation, and so it was hardly surprising that they started going in their droves to the ballrooms to dance the night away. A fair percentage of the crowd probably even harboured the dream of meeting Mister or Miss Right in those ballrooms.

Each of these venues had their own Musicians' Union controlled big band, providing the backdrop to the endless chat-up lines and supplying the soundtrack to many a budding romance. The bands we're talking about here all worked under the name of their leader, like The Joe Loss Orchestra – who released a staggering 110 singles on the HMV label of which only five made their way to the dizzy heights of the Top 50. (They peaked with 'The Maigret Theme' achieving number 20 in March 1962.) Other successful orchestras included The Victor Sylvester Orchestra, The Billy Cotton Band, Ivy Benson & Her Orchestra, The Ted Heath Band, Jack Hylton & His Orchestra (in 1929 he played a staggering 700 gigs and sold three million records and was still going strong during the late Forties and early Fifties), Johnny Douglas & His Orchestra, Ray Martin & His Orchestra, Frank Weir, His Saxophone, His Chorus *and* (if you don't mind) His Orchestra, and, later on, Ken McIntosh and Ray McVay. Mostly these bands played what was known as the Mecca circuit.

In 1946 people were obviously anxious to get out of their houses because an absolutely staggering 1,635,000,000 cinema tickets were sold in the UK! The feel-good factor, the sense of liberation after five grim years of war, certainly extended beyond the silver screen, with dancers flocking in record numbers to see and hear all sorts of live music.

At this stage, though, the dancers, for their part, had eyes only for each other and pretty much ignored the efforts of the musicians up on the stage.

Eyes only for each other that was until towards the end of the Forties, when people like Johnny Dankworth's Big Band became so popular that on their nights off from the resident gigs they were invited to perform in other ballrooms. By this time, the battle, which had started in the late Twenties between popular music (waltz and foxtrot) and hot music (jazz), had been won outright by jazz, although the more famous popular music orchestras and big bands waltzed on successfully until well into the Sixties. Generally the big bands would have performed with "a take it or leave it" attitude, but Dankworth's boys had more spunk in that they weren't just working musicians reading the dots for the MU scale. They positively loved their traditional style of jazz, and it showed in the enthusiasm they put into the performance.

The Original Dixieland Jazz Bands made their first jazz recordings in 1917. "Jazz" was an 1880's black slang word for "sexual activity and excitement", so you can see what was turning both the musicians and dancers on. By the end of 1926 the dance band era was slowly making way for the jazz and blues era. Due to the absolute devastation of the two world wars and the loss of many great musicians, it took until the mid-Forties for things to get back in gear again. Its growth was helped in no small way by BBC Radio, which started broadcasting on November 14, 1922; television, which started in 1930 but didn't make an impression until it resumed in 1946 following the WWII blackout; and movies which when they progressed to talkies in the Thirties provided a valuable springboard for new music.

As far as the audiences were concerned the musicians' passion was infectious, and soon Dankworth and some of his contemporaries like The Ronnie Scott Band and The Chris Barber Band, were building a large following for both their live appearances and their record releases. Dankworth was Musician of the Year in *Melody Maker* jazz poll every year from 1949 to 1955. The jazz bands, including people like Acker Bilk and Kenny Ball, grew from the numerous jazz clubs springing up all over the place and then they progressed to the dance halls. All the bands travelled together in the band bus, and were accompanied by a band boy – the prototype roadie.

The jazz movement, and momentum, was to be seriously derailed by a man from within its own ranks. The jazz era had always suffered, or

benefited – it's always hard to be sure which – from the internal con-
flicts of Trad over Modern, or New Orleans over Be-Bop, but no one
could have guessed that it would be overtaken by a new form of music,
originally used as intermission music for their own shows.

Lonnie Donegan was The Chris Barber Band's banjo player. He had
swagger and he had style but, truth be told, he would probably have
been just as happy to have continued in the Barber band. However, in
1956, towards the end of one of the Barber recording sessions, Donegan
recorded an up-tempo song by US bluesman Leadbelly called 'Rock
Island Line' and Skiffle music was born. Well, maybe not so much born
– because Skiffle roots can be traced to earlier – as thrown out onto the
streets as a screaming teenager.

Skiffle was a fusion of black rhythms and English folk music. Radio
picked up on the album track, which, as we've said, had been an afterthought. Decca Records, by all accounts begrudgingly, released it as a
single. Although it peaked at number two in the charts, it became the
first debut single to sell a million and went on to sell three million copies
worldwide, for which Lonnie received the princely sum of three
pounds and ten shillings (£3.50). Lonnie was the first artist to be
awarded a Gold Disc for hitting a million sales on his debut disc. Over
the following years he had hits with 'Putting On The Style', 'Have A
Drink On Me', 'Michael Row The Boat Ashore', 'My Old Man's A
Dustman', 'Does Your Chewing Gum Lose Its Flavour', 'Battle Of
New Orleans' and 'Pick A Bale Of Cotton'. He was the first artist to
have an album sell in such vast quantities that it qualified for a position
in the more rarefied air of the singles charts. He inspired a very young
Phil Spector to take up guitar and even the great Taj Mahal has admitted
to being influenced by his early records.

Lonnie Donegan set a lot of landmark records, which The Beatles
eventually broke. It's worth noting that the earlier vision of the Fab
Four was also a skiffle outfit called The Quarrymen. But let's stay with
Lonnie for a few more moments. He was the Oasis and the Bruce
Springsteen, rolled into one, of his day. But more importantly for us,
he single-handedly breathed vital life into the contemporary music
touring circuit. He set the foundations for the beat boom with his
electrifying performances. He toured the UK, playing cinemas, dance
halls, ballrooms, music halls and the Moss Empire theatre circuit,
sometimes playing as many as four performances a day. Lonnie
enjoyed ticket sales in excess of 250,000 for a three-month tour, when
tours weren't really tours but a series of never-ending one-nighters.

Cities would come to a standstill when he hit town.

It's important to realise that Lonnie Donegan was probably the first UK artist in the popular music field who wasn't a poor imitation of an American original. While in the crooning game the US had Frank Sinatra and Dean Martin, the UK had Dickie Valentine and Frankie Vaughan. It's also interesting to note that although Lonnie enjoyed considerable success in America, the skiffle movement as a whole didn't make much impact there.

Before we go much further here, we need to name-check Les Paul. He'd approached The Gibson Company (famous for their acoustic guitars and mandolins) as early as the Forties, with his revolutionary ideas for a solid electric guitar. He didn't see his dream come true though until 1952 – when coincidentally he was the most popular guitarist in the USA – and Gibson launched the Les Paul model guitar. Though Leo Fender entered the market soon after, first with his Broadcaster/Telecaster and then the revolutionary Stratocaster, the solid guitar hasn't changed much since then, except that they've improved the bridge and pickups. Under its current market name, The Les Paul Standard, it is as popular as it ever was. Even today it still looks sleek and sexy, so you can imagine what people thought of it in the Fifties. On top of which, it consistently sounded great and gave the fledgling pop stars greater on-stage mobility.

Back in England though, the venues, which were welcoming Lonnie with open arms, were shortly thereafter booking the graduates of London's 2Is Club in Old Compton Street. This black box basement, with a pair of eyes painted (by Lionel Bart) above the stage, had become the breeding ground for the Larry Parnes stable of stars. We're talking about artists like Joe Brown, Billy Fury, Marty Wilde, Tommy Steele, Georgie Fame, who along with Cliff Richard and Adam Faith, were heading up the Elvis the UK pelvis movement. That is to say they were bridging the gap between the English based skiffle sound and the embryonic rock'n'roll of the USA, with a sharp violent swing of the hips. "Rock'n'roll" was yet another set of slang words for sexual activity, and juke box owners reported in 1955 that they were using 60% more rock'n'roll and R&B discs than they had the previous year. Even though Elvis Presley and Bill Hailey had joined the bestseller lists, radio, believe it or not, resisted playing their records on the grounds that playing records live, on air, potentially deprived working musicians from earning a living. Up to then, obviously encouraged sternly by the MU, musicians performed music on radio live.

8

Fortunately, just before the MU, the BBC and the music publishers – the Holy Trinity in the fledgling UK music business – had a chance to stifle the birth of rock'n'roll, along came television producer Jack Good who stuck the 2Is set on a Saturday night prime-time TV show called *6.5 Special*. Later he moved over to the infant ITV with *Oh Boy*. These two vital television slots made stars out of the Cliffs, the Tommys, the Billys and the Joes and in the late Fifties, early Sixties, they all hit the road with a vengeance, filling every Top Rank venue in the country. Eventually even the ABC cinema chain also opened their doors to the new stars.

They toured mostly in "packages", which was probably a spillover from the days when the orchestras toured and would have several vocalists to entertain the audience during the course of an evening. A typical package would consist of five or six acts who would invariably all use the same drum kit, a Vox AC50 amp (for the bass) and a couple of Vox AC30s (plus a spare if you were lucky) for the guitars. They would use the house public address (PA) system, which was probably why the audience had a hard time hearing the lyrics. Vocalists would get paid £40, musicians £20 and roadies £10. The star of the show would play for 20 minutes, second on the bill would play 15 minutes and the others would get 10 minutes each. The cinemas these packages played in were used to a more docile crowd, so the hysteria generated by the new crowds reacting to their favourite gyrating stars tended to be well covered in the national papers. This all served to further fuel the fire of the already growing movement. The acts would do two and sometimes four shows a day and between shows the musicians could be seen dallying around the stage door area with the local scrubbers.

The problem with rock'n'roll stars was that in order to maintain their profile among young, predominantly teenage fans, they had to sell records in sufficient quantities without appearing to be aiming for a wider, adult market. Sadly, Lonnie Donegan and Tommy Steele faltered and fell at this hurdle. Somehow they were persuaded to do (the then popular) gimmicky singles such as 'Does Your Chewing Gum Lose Its Flavour On Your Bedpost Over Night?' (Lonnie) and 'Little White Bull' (Tommy). Mr. Steele *even* appeared in pantomime. Oh yes he did. All of which served to lose both artists credibility and a good proportion of their live audience. Both eventually recovered to some degree, but it could be argued that neither fully realised the potential each of them had hinted at in the first flush of their success.

Whatever the failings of the home-grown species, the British

9

rock'n'roll scene had a shot in the arm whenever package tours of American rock'n'rollers hit the theatres. Barring Elvis, all the top names made the pilgrimage and the reaction was bedlam all round. Then, at the cusp of the Fifties and into the early Sixties, there was a strange lull, as if the music industry establishment had won and taken control again. What they hadn't reckoned on was the seeds the American rock'n'rollers had sown among the next generation of British teenagers.

So it was that from 1963 onwards The Beatles and another revolutionary television show called *Ready Steady Go!*, shepherded in the Beat Group Boom with groups such as The Kinks, The Yardbirds, The Animals, The Who, The Rolling Stones and Them forming the core. All these and other such bands lived in their Ford Transit or Comer vans while playing in every city, town and village that had a link to the M1 or the A1. The circuit and system (packages) was pretty much a progression from above save that the scrubbers were now called groupies.

The Beatles, of course, were not a poor imitation of an American original, and because of this they opened up the American market to all those who were sufficiently skilled or original to follow in their wake. This upped the ante considerably and certainly went a long way towards establishing the music industry as it is today – a big business and a playground of opportunity for sharp entrepreneurs.

Then came the Underground, spearheaded by groups like Taste, Spooky Tooth, Free, Jethro Tull, 10 Years After, The Nice, Yes, Genesis, Cream and ELP, who moved out of the now thriving club circuit into the colleges. Some of the Sixties groups such as The Kinks, The Who, Pink Floyd and The Moody Blues survived, and enjoyed continued success on this very credible circuit. Each university had its entertainments committee of bright students, many of whom would go on to become agents, managers and record company executives to the thriving music industry, which was, as it always had been, based in London.

And in 1977 just when we were getting used to that, along came the punks to shake everything up. Though it seemed at the time as if the punks had appeared from nowhere, they had actually received an unexpected leg-up from the pub rock movement. The important thing with all new movements is youth and looks, but the pub rock movement was comprised of either old men with beards playing R&B and classics or young men in beards pretending to be old men in beards playing R&B and classics. Either way, by the time the punks – with their R&B based sound – arrived on the scene, the pub rock bands were on their last legs. When the punks weren't allowed access to the progressive clubs, they inherited and developed the back-room-of-pubs circuit. When they had outgrown that, there was a new wave of social secretaries to welcome them into their colleges and universities. Then the Top Rank circuit opened their doors to this enthusiastic, gobbing audience and the focus of their attention. We're talking here about The Stranglers, The Clash, The Undertones, The Banshees, The Buzzcocks, The Gang Of 4, The Lurkers and a host of others.

The punks might have stormed the barricades but they didn't see off the dinosaurs for the simple reason that their audience was never going to go away. In fact they became new wave but by this time things had settled down again and just about everyone, balladeers and rockers alike, were all simply filed under 'rock' (certainly without the roll). These new larger-than-life acts, those that had stayed the pace, benefited greatly from the larger-than-life arenas like Wembley, Birmingham NEC, Manchester G Mex, Newcastle Arena, Glasgow SEC and then, when even these establishments proved to be too humble, the rock artists progressed into football stadiums.

Sadly there have been no major musical changes since then. Yes, of course there have been lots of new and successful artists, but for ages now nobody has really offered anything different to what's come before. So the circuit has pretty much stabilised, save that the old-style Music Halls and theatres are slowly but surely making way for the newer multi-purpose and multi-style civic halls which are, it has to be said, facility-wise, as good as it gets.

And there, and here, we are.

2

GETTING STARTED

Okay, I hope you're settling in. You've picked up the knowledge on how the circuit started. Now it's your turn. I can tell you want to get on to that circuit.

And you'll probably find that although all you really want to do is write songs and perform them on stage, you're having difficulty getting started. From the outside, the music business, with all its apparently trendy and super cool people, its buzzwords, its in-phrases and jargon, can appear quite intimidating; but the reality is that from the inside it's really quite basic and very simple.

"Oh, right, that's the secret then," I hear you say. "I didn't know it was *that* simple. I'll knock out a couple of tunes this afternoon and get started on my career immediately. Then this very afternoon I'll write a cheque against my future earnings and send it off to Messrs Gibson for a brand new Les Paul."

Aye, if only it *were* that simple and if only it were that easy, because we all know it's not easy climbing any slippery pole. I have to tell you, I know few who work as hard as artists when they are Playing Live and involved in all the arrangements that go with it.

An average day can be something like:

07.00: Check out of hotel.
07.30: Wait outside hotel in bus for 30 minutes while the tour manager wakes up the drummer.
08.00: Drive to airport.
09.00: Check in at airport.
10.00: Fly to next city.
11.00: Arrive at next city.

12

11.30: Picked up at airport by the record company's local promotional person and driven to local radio station.

12.00: Arrive at radio station to do interview.

13.00: Drive to local television studio, accompanied by journalist who interviews you on the way.

13.30: Arrive at television station. Go straight to make-up.

13.45: Interviewed live on television then perform single using a strange guitar.

14.00: Photo session and interview for local evening newspaper in television studio car park.

14.30: Drive to another radio station, enjoying egg sandwich and cold coffee en route.

15.15: Live on air.

15.30: Drive to hotel while conducting four- to five-minute press interviews on your mobile on the way.

16.10: Arrive at hotel. Rushed straight to room for an hour of European phoners (interviews).

17.15: Depart hotel for gig.

17.30: Arrive at gig and proceed straight to sound check.

18.45: Conclude sound check and go straight to catering.

19.30: Move to dressing room, undertake more phoners this time with American press and radio stations.

20.15: Meet with MD of your record company who can't stay until the end of your show, something to do with a baby-sitter or was that maybe about doing a baby-sitter.

20.30: On stage.

22.30: Off stage.

22.30 to 22.35: Bliss! Nothing to do. The first real break of the day.

22.35: The meet and greet with record company executives, local radio station producers, DJs, journalists, local record store staff and (hopefully) family.

23.05: Meet fans at stage door and sign autographs.

23.40: Late night Indian meal with record company executives.

01.30: Return to hotel. Meet up with the band in the bar for a few drinks.

02.20: Retire to bedroom to take 20 minutes of American calls.

04.20: Alarm call.

05.00: Taken to local television station for Breakfast Television appearance.

And then it starts all over again.

"Brilliant," I hear you scream, "he waits until we've bought the book, taken it home and *then* he tells us that bit."

Yes, but it's important to be aware that the above is an extract from a well-known star's itinerary and you know what? They don't begrudge it one bit because the majority of those I have had the privilege of working with know that you don't sell tickets and records by accident. It really is 10% inspiration and 90% perspiration.

Anyway, we're getting ahead of ourselves here, so let's go back to how this artist or any typical artist actually gets started.

Most of the artists I meet, who are starting on the road to Playing Live, would give their eye-teeth to be in the above artist's high-heeled shoes. You know, to be in a position where they can have a career and make at least a comfortable enough living from writing and performing their songs to an adoring and receptive audience.

Their first audience would have been their bedroom mirror – a perfect if somewhat less than discerning start. The first of many important points is to get your music, your songs and your act together, away from prying eyes.

Always, do it away from the public glare.

Okay, so we'll start with the songs, because that is the *only* real place to start.

Find something you *need* to say about love, about life, about politics about . . . subterranean homesick blues . . . about yellow paper taxis . . . or the viaducts of your dreams . . . about anything, anything at all just as long as it's something that moves you. Then find your own set of musical colours to set your thoughts to. Craft your songs, waste not a word, make every word count and do it all when the song is new to you. Get in, say what you want to say and get out as soon as possible; it worked for The Beatles, it'll work for you.

For the sake of our book, let's assume you've got your songs together. The next thing you have to think about is how you intend to perform them. Your options are either to go solo or to form a band. Well, it's not strictly true, those are your only two options if you write and want to perform your own songs. The third, and less stressful option, applies when you only want to be a songwriter and not a performer.

Bob McDill is one of my favourite songwriters and yet I don't think he's ever done a gig in his life. If you feel you're similarly disinclined, you don't need an agent, just make a demo tape and send your songs to a music publisher.

But assuming you do have ambitions to be a performer as well as a writer then solo is obviously the most cost-effective way to start. The wage bill is relatively small and you're not going to moan at yourself for not paying yourself your own money on time. However, if you do intend to work solo, you are leaving a lot of the interpretation of your music to the imagination of the music business. I wouldn't do that if I were you. Even if you don't want to have a democratic band, you should still consider using a few other musicians to flesh out your sound so that the version of your music people hear is as close as possible to the finished version of your music that you hear in your head. If you are forming a band, then it's much easier for you at this stage. Your problems will come later.

Choosing a professional name is probably the next important part of our process. The name of your group is important, but probably not vitally important. I remember sitting down with John Illsley and David Knopfler and trying to convince them that they might want to change the name of their group. I know, I know, yes they did record one of the biggest albums of all time, but you have to admit it wasn't one of the most inspiring of names ever chosen by a group of musicians.

Names sometimes can take on an alternative meaning. I mean I've often thought that "Also Appearing", "Plus Special Guest" or "Plus Support" would be a great name for a group. You just imagine people saying, "They must be a great band that Plus Support crowd, they're playing absolutely everywhere!" Or Marks & Sparks: I always thought that would be a good one, it's already in most people's consciousness. It might even open some sponsorship opportunities for you. The other thing to remember is that it's important that it's easy for people to be able to spell and pronounce your name. Your name is only important until you achieve some degree of success then, just as was the case with Dire Straits, people will be so into your music they won't care a fig about what you're called.

So we have *our* name. For the sake of this book let's call our group Goggles Anonymous. We have our songs, we have our musicians, now it's time to start rehearsing and rehearsing and then rehearsing a wee bit more. Around the time boredom is setting in, you should plan your first appearance; say about three months ahead. It will be the prospect of that appearance that will see you through the next three months of rehearsals.

After you've got your sound together non-stop rehearsals don't really benefit you – don't forget if it's brittle it breaks.

15

For your first performance, you should pick somewhere off the beaten track, and invite only friends, family and lovers. If you're an out-of-work musician, you are going to be pretty low on the first and last of those three categories, so make sure there's at least one Irish member in your group, to ensure that you'll have a big crowd in the family category.

Do your gig and *have fun*. That's the single most important part of all of this – **have fun**. If you're having fun and enjoying what you do, it tends to be pretty infectious, so there's a good chance the audience will have fun too. Oh yes, and record the gig. Don't bother booking an expensive mobile unit – something cheap and cheerful will do.

Listen to your tape. Separate your heart from the songs and listen to the performance. Go through the live tape, song by song, listening as closely to the audience's reaction as to the performance of the songs. Audiences never lie; they can't. No matter how enthusiastic they may want to be because they know you, when you listen to their applause on tape, you'll hear very clearly which songs worked and which songs didn't. Start rehearsing again, and then, just like last time, schedule another show for say two or three months down the line.

If you were really happy with the quality of your first performance, this time expand the audience beyond your immediate group of friends. Hire the upstairs or back room of a pub. You'll be surprised by how reasonable landlords will be when they realise you are going to bring 10, 20, 30, 50, 100 drinkers into their pub. Print wee flyers and tickets. I bet at least one member of your band will be a computer genius and she, or he, will have a computer programme that will print up multicoloured flyers. Keep them simple, keep them classy and try to find a way to include a few hints in art and words that will allude to the essence of your music. Throw in a wee bit of mystery as well – that always works wonders. Have your band and all your mates sell tickets to all of *their* mates. It's the networking theory and it's been proven to work wonders again and again.

In your spare time, find a way to get a bit of studio experience. Go to the nearest recording studios, tell them you'll make the tea, you'll sweep the floor, you'll do absolutely anything. Even go as far as to say you'll work for free. Anything, as long as you can get in there and see how a recording studio works. Save your home recording experimentations until later. Latch on to an engineer and be his runner, his assistant, his anything, just to get a chance to see him in action with a real group. See if you can hang on part-time for about six months or so, and learn, learn and then learn some more.

At the same time as you're rehearsing, selling tickets for your next show, writing songs and getting studio experience, see if you can also secure some work as a roadie. You can do this either by seeking work with Stage Miracles, who supply the load-in and load-out teams for the majority of the London promoters, or, preferably, go on the road as a roadie with a professional band. Use the opportunity to get your hands dirty and see how things really work from the inside. Pretty soon you will realise that all is rarely how it might seem. The politics of a band on the road are intriguing and if you know what to expect further down the line, you can head a few potential problems off at the pass.

Let's assume this is all about Playing Live. Everything you now do is a means to an end to playing live. This means that making records and videos, appearing on television and radio and general media involvement are all a by-product of getting up on a concert stage somewhere in the world 100 to 200 nights per year.

I mention this because, in many instances, live concert appearances are not considered to be the central part of an artist's career, but another vehicle by which to promote the records. Some people do this because they have to, it's a vocation, they were born to write and sing their songs. Others do it because it's another way to promote their albums. To them it's a necessary by-product of being in the music *business*. *Playing Live*, the book, by virtue of its title I hope tells you on which side my bread has been buttered.

So, Goggles Anonymous are starting out; learning their craft. Now it's time to start to look outside the band and consider some of the other people you'll have to work with to get on the road professionally.

Even if your preference is to be a gigging musician, you'll still want to secure a recording deal to release versions of your songs to your fans and a publishing deal to protect your songs and collect your worldwide income on them.

How do you secure these deals?

Okay, here's one of the big secrets coming. In the majority of cases, record companies, agents, managers and music publishers are alike. They like to discover their acts. They like to tap into something already in existence. Something that has, to some degree, proven that it has legs. They like to feel it's something they can't afford to ignore.

You have to realise that all these professionals receive CDs and cassettes from hundreds of artists each and every week of their lives and they know there is a good chance that their colleagues are receiving the exact same packages. Most of them don't really listen to the music they're sent. They employ an office junior to do their listening for them. The chance of someone hearing your CD or cassette and doing something about it are about 1 in 3,849. (That statistic is based on the fact that 89% of statistics are made up on the spot.) So, what you have to do is find an alternative route into their consciousness, to avoid being lumped in with a mountain of other music under consideration.

When The Kinks were starting out in the Sixties, they came up with a simple but effective idea which has been repeated with varying degrees of success ever since. When they started, they only played at parties and events. They appeared to be playing their own little exclusive circuit, when in fact the reality was the posh parties were the only gigs their managers had the contacts for. But by playing thus, they separated themselves from the majority of bands. In creating their own little scene they started to develop a following. By doing this, and doing it successfully, you start a buzz. That is to say, you start people in the music business talking about you.

Next you have friends of friends drop the word into key record company executives ears, "Pssst, you want to get down to the Dublin Castle in Camden Town to *check out* this amazing new group."

It works every time, the key words are "check" and "out", but they have to be used together.

The record executive goes to the gig, all of his competitors are already there and he thinks, "How come they're already on to this?" He just sees all these other people, convinces himself even before the group has come on the stage that something is happening there and immediately he's interested.

If you have a band, it's important you all look like you're in the same group. Say, for instance, you superimposed an image of one of The Rolling Stones into a photograph of The Beatles, there'd be no problem, or prizes for, spotting the odd one out. Exactly the same would apply if you planted a Beatle amongst the Stones. The look has to be natural though, it has to come from within and not from the pages of a stylist's back copies of *Fab 208*. There is a good chance that someone within your ranks will be preoccupied with the look and will shape the visual style of the band, maybe even just by example, if you'll let them. Be careful though, I'm sure someone from within the ranks of the US grunge movement at one point must have thought they looked cool, but look where that led us?

Yes, it's great being individual, but you're at an even bigger advantage if you're individual *and* you're part of a movement. There's safety *and* power in numbers.

Anyway, now you have your audience, your circuit, your sound, your look, your name, and the ears of the music industry, it's down to you and to your songs. And the magic of doing it this way is that you don't have to get started by playing every dive in England, third on the bill, then second on the bill and, rarely if ever, top of the bill. That's certainly the way it used to happen, but it seldom happens that way any more. These days, it's just as effective, and a lot less expensive, to play one key date a month, as long as you make the date work for you. If you have everything in place and your act together (figuratively and artistically speaking) you'll get your record deal and be on your way. But please remember, you are just one more step on your way. A lot of people make the mistake of thinking that once they have a record deal, they're made. Not so. It's important if you go this route that you don't forget the audience you have started to build up, keep working at it, maybe spread your wings a little further afield and develop other areas so you are not overplaying your strong area. The important part in all of this is to try and have an audience waiting for your first record by the time it comes out; that way you have a head start on the majority of acts.

Putting your band together can be tricky, but not quite as tricky if you take care to spend time and attention and manage to get things set up properly at the start. Let's address the band situation before we move to the next step.

3

THE BAND

The music business – like most other sections of the entertainment industry I suppose – is littered with artists who never really quite made it and still don't know how to give up. Put someone on a stage, some-where, anywhere, and someone will turn up to watch and listen to them perform. And this is all the encouragement most of these artists need to continue. They are prepared to sacrifice their health, their wealth, their heart and their lives to be allowed to bask in the spotlight. It doesn't matter whether the light be from a 60-watt bulb at the Half Moon in Putney, or, from 20 Super Trooper spotlights at Wembley Arena.

These artists and their entourages – musicians, managers, agents, roadies, parents, wives, boyfriends, girlfriends, lawyers, accountants – continually intrigue me, and I've been working in this area for 30 years now. Why do they keep going? Why do they never achieve the success of some of their contemporaries? Some certainly have a body of work deserving greater success. I'm equally intrigued by how musicians come together to form a band; how the hierarchy of the band is decided in the first few months of the band's life. For instance, if Brian Jones hadn't lost out in the power struggle with Andrew Loog Oldham in The Rolling Stones wars, then perhaps they'd be more a Chicken Skin Music type of band than the Granddaddy of Rock they've become.

In one of my crime novels, *The Ballad of Sean & Wilco*, I really enjoyed putting together my own fictitious group, The Circles, and surrounding them with a team of characters. But you'll probably find that my fictitious dream team will never be as unpredictable as your very own real team.

In the all-important first few months of putting your group together, you'll note the initial shuffling of feet as your band members jockey for position. Again, potentially, these are the people whose pockets you are going to live in for the next five years or so – maybe even as much as the following two or three decades. So, my advice is to observe your colleagues closely and replace the troublesome members immediately. It will be much easier to do it in the initial stage, rather than waiting a few years when they're sharing the spotlight with you. The infamous firing of Pete Best nearly de-railed The Beatles from their mega successful path.

One of the guys in Fruupp (my first management client) liked to drink a bit too much. He was a sweetheart when sober but a right royal pain in the posterior when he had a few on him. What I'm saying is that we, the other musicians and myself, might have saved ourselves a lot of anguish and frustration if we'd parted company in the very early days. Who knows, we might even have been a lot more successful than we were.

Talking about Fruupp again reminds me of another important point – knowing when to quit. In Goggles Anonymous there might just come a time when you have to face the truth and realise that you aren't getting anywhere and it might be time to call it a day.

With Fruupp, we were a bunch of good mates. There was Martin Foye on drums, Peter Farrelly on bass and vocals, Vincent McCusker on guitars, Stephen Houston on keyboards, John Urry & Litz the roadies and yours truly doing everything else. They were a good group. They spent quite a time on the circuit (five years) and then, just when it appeared we were starting to make some progress on that slippery slope, Stephen discovered God and (quite literally and uncharitably) disappeared overnight.

Now, as part of the typical knee-jerk reaction, we all closed ranks and declared, "We'll show him. We'll show him we don't need him." And so we soldiered on, when in fact we shouldn't have. We should have taken stock and realised – what Stephen had probably realised but couldn't bring himself to admit to us – that we weren't going to happen and if we hadn't made progress with our third album, *The Prince Of Heaven's Eyes*, which was by far our finest moment, then we weren't going to break through at all.

So, we replaced him, made another album but the inevitable split came a couple of years later.

But I was there and I can tell you, when you're in the thick of it, it's hard to make that call. You play a great gig, the audience sends you home feeling 10 feet tall and once again you're convinced that you're on the right track. So you stay on that track for the following few months. On top of which, you keep reminding yourself that you've invested a good chunk of your life in this band. Even if you manage to put that out of your mind, you'll certainly start to think, "What else can I find to do to pay the rent?" So you keep at it, because in the music business there's always somewhere to play, there's always someone who'll put out your music and there are always people who will come to see you. There are always people who will write about you and talk about your music and play it on the radio. The big hungry music business machine needs feeding and it doesn't insist on all its meals being gourmet.

No matter what they tell you at LIPA, there are no exams you can take which will guarantee your success in the music business and playing live. No one really knows about this stuff, so how could anyone teach it to you.

If Goggles Anonymous doesn't make it, there's nothing to say that should lead singer, Philip Dansette, go solo (with similar material) he wouldn't become mega. Hey, it might not even be Philip; it might even be the drummer. Still, the band would be well advised to keep an eye on things and not be scared of considering their long-term future.

When you're putting your band together, choose your fellow travellers wisely, that's all I'm saying. To some degree it's easier if you want to be a solo artist. You can hire and fire your musicians as you need them. Talking about musicians and drummers . . .

Drummers generally are the butt of jokes. For example, how do you get rid of the drummer at your door? Pay for the Pizza. What do you call a drummer who's just been dumped by his girlfriend? Homeless. And on and on they go. But seriously, there was this drummer and he'd had enough of such jokes and so he decided that much and all as he loved drumming he was going to take up some other instruments as well. He felt were he to learn to play at least two other instruments then he'd be taken more seriously by his peers and he'd enjoy a lot more credibility as a musician.

Secretly he sets off into town one morning in to the local music store. He walks into the store, let's call it Crymbals, and there are rows and rows of beautiful guitars, pianos, saxophones, clarinets, trombones, trumpets, accordions, oboes, flutes and organs. Our drummer walks around the store for about half an hour, trying to work out which of the instruments will be easiest to master so that he can earn his credibility points.

Eventually he reaches his decision.

"Yes," he says to the friendly assistant, pointing up to the wall behind him, "I'd like to buy that red trumpet and," he continues, pointing to another corner of the store, "that cream accordion over there."

"Ah," says the assistant, "whereas most of the items in the store are for sale Sir, I'm afraid that red fire extinguisher and the cream radiator are not!"

Boom Boom.

I think drummers receive such stick because generally they are so desperate for success that most of them will play with several bands in the hope that at least one of them will succeed.

The ability to make it or succeed is relative anyway, isn't it? If you're working in a day job and playing guitar with your mates at weekends, then a musician making a full-time living by playing music could be deemed, by you, to have made it. But then, such a musician will look higher up the pecking order and his wish will be to want to be in a band that not only plays live for a living, but who also visits the recording studio and puts out records. Then, if you are in that lofty position, not only will you want to be putting out records, you'll also want to be selling them in sufficient quantities to enter the sales charts and so on and so forth.

And sometimes bands and artists fail to make it, not because of what they are doing musically, but due to the human weakness of one, or some, in their midst.

Take Stevie Ray Vaughan for instance.

A chap called Chesley Millington, who used to do PR for The Chieftains in America, rang me up one day out of the blue. A mutual friend, David Lindley, had given him my number. Chesley was a real character, cut from the old (high quality) cloth, he would ring up newspapers with the line, "Hold the front page, I've got a great story for you." Honestly! *And* he'd get his stories in.

He rang me because he wanted me to listen to his "amazing" new act, "A kid," (his words) he'd discovered playing guitar in Texas. He duly sent me a tape and he was spot on. The guitarist on the tape was on fire and he sounded to me like he'd really be great live too. Chesley was wheeling and dealing and had the interest of a few record companies, but an important part of his plan, he explained, was not to wait for American success before hitting Europe, but to start to build up "The Kid's" profile in Europe at the same time.

Anyway, Stevie and his fine band, Double Trouble, signed to CBS/Sony and enjoyed considerable success quite quickly. Within a few years he was very big on the European concert circuit. But like a lot of quiet introspective musicians who strive for success, they discover when they reach the dizzy heights that it wasn't what they'd dreamed of. Sometimes the pressure is quite unbearable. Artists generally start off because they love writing songs and singing and playing live and that's certainly fine. Yep that's okay, but it doesn't necessarily mean that they're going to be okay doing the meet and greets. It doesn't mean that they're going to bear putting up with everyone around them wanting a little piece of them and then wanting to protect that little piece, sometimes at the artist's cost. It doesn't mean that they're going to be comfortable with the media trail. It's really very unnatural and can be quite alien to those of a sensitive nature.

Sometimes when you reach the plateau of your career, you'll realise that Dylan was spot on when he sang: *And don't go mistaking paradise for that place across the road.* And when paradise isn't all you expect or need, like Adam and Eve, you'll be tempted to grasp at the forbidden fruit for your answer.

It's not that I'm trying to justify any such actions; it's just that I met Stevie Ray Vaughan and I always found him to be a beautiful sweet man. A Southern American Gentleman in fact. And, like Rory Gallagher, if anything Stevie was a painfully shy man.

Sadly, at the peak of his success, Stevie found the need to turn to medication to help him through the night only to find that the remedy proved to be the poison. It all ended very sadly.

I remember he'd been ill, but he'd cleaned up his act, had a new lady in his life, found religion and arrived over here for a seven week European tour which started with a sold out show in Paris. During the Paris performance, his demons came back to haunt him and he lost it while on stage. He went into these long monologues, leaving his band and crew, not to mention the audience, very confused. He had to be checked into hospital that night and the rest of the tour was cancelled. Sadly, even though he enjoyed a lot of good times after that, the damage was done and he passed away several months later.

You look at this and similar tragic stories and, even considering the great legacy left behind, you'd have to say that even with all the success achieved, in those instances it's just not worth it. Nothing's worth giving your life for. But it's never made easy for you because, as the saying goes: "The devil always arrives bearing the largest cheques."

Be careful.

*

The other issue that needs to be sorted out at the formation stage is the financial infrastructure of your band. Again, if you are a solo act, at least on paper, it's pretty simple. You write the songs, you hire musicians to help you perform and record them, so you receive all the money, right? No, it's not always as simple as that.

"Sorry?"

Not always.

"But surely?"

Okay, say you write a song, a great song for the sake of this discussion, and you go into the studio with a bunch of musicians to record your masterpiece. During the recording, the saxophone player comes up with this amazing head-turning intro(duction) to the recording of your song, or the guitarist plays a classic guitar solo to fill the gap in the middle of your song. Nothing more is thought of it until the record comes out and begins to storm its way up the charts all over the world. The money starts to roll in. That's when the trouble starts. You see, when a hired musician plays on a record, he or she receives a flat (Musician's Union approved) payment. It doesn't (in theory) matter to him, or her, if the record sells 10 copies to your family members or 10 million copies to a growing army of fans worldwide. However, the closer the figure is to 10 million, the higher the chances that, all of a sudden, the saxophone player will claim he wrote the intro and that it was the intro that became the hook and the reason that the song was such a hit and, wait for it, yes, the reason he should receive some of the publishing royalties. The guitarist will chip into the discussion that, "Well really, it's not much of a song if you take the guitar solo out and hey, I'm due a share of the royalties too."

The simple solution is to have the musicians sign a receipt when they are being paid for their recording services saying, "for full and final settlement." Equally, if you should happen to be either the saxophone player or the guitar player in the above situation, deal with it immediately. If you come up with an original contribution to the song, make your feelings known immediately and if you can't come to an agreement, advise them that you'd prefer that your work be removed from the track.

Sting was invited by Mark Knopfler to come down to the studio to sing guest vocals on one of Dire Straits' records. Sting's contribution to the song was so distinctively Sting, that, near enough on the spot, Mark gave him a co-writer credit and a share of the publishing rights on the song. The song was 'Money For Nothing' and the situation was dealt with correctly and very professionally so all concerned were perfectly pleased when it became the worldwide smash hit it did.

In a band set-up, it's never quite as simple as that. For instance, even though you have a band where all members are equal partners, you will still have someone who writes the majority, if not all, of the material. So you all slog around the country for years trying to make ends meet, preaching the gospel according to the writer's songs, and building up an audience. The audience arrives and the albums start to sell and then, suddenly, one in your midst (the songwriter) starts to receive a lot more money than the rest of you. It's extremely hard to feel equal at that stage. He moves into a mansion in Chelsea, while you purchase a flat in Clapton; he drives round in a Jaguar S Type, while you have to make do with your Fiat Punto. No matter how good a mate he once was, no matter how aware you are that he writes all the songs, you're still going to feel pissed off and your feeling pissed off can be the fatal crack in the dyke.

On the other hand if you give your non-songwriting fellow band members a piece of your songs, eventually you're going to resent them, particularly when, and if, the band splits up and they're still receiving a percentage of your songs.

How do you get over this particularly spiked hurdle?

The Beatles got over it by giving George and Ringo a percentage of their publishing company, Northern Songs. George eventually started to come up with a Northern Song or two of his own, and classics they were too. For other solutions check what other bands do by looking at the songwriting credits on album sleeves. The Doors, Rockpile and U2, for example, make interesting reading.

There is just one further bit of advice I'd like to give you before we move away from the songwriting side of things. When, and if, you have your first hit, you are going to be totally gobsmacked by the number of people who will come out of the woodwork. I have to tell you that there are some sad and sorry people out there who will convince themselves and others that they have written your hit song. I'm sure you've witnessed some very famous cases in the press. Now of course *we* all know that you are the songwriter and the song has come from your pen and your pen alone, but a judge will not simply take your word for it. You are going to have to take time out of your busy schedule and employ a legal team to address this issue. So, my tip is each and every time you write a song, record it onto a cassette, place the cassette in an envelope with a handwritten copy of the lyrics including any changes and any wee notes or documents which might show where you got the ideas for your song. Seal the package, write on the outside of the envelope the title(s) of the song(s) included and send it back to yourself by registered post. This process will date and time your work. When you receive the package in the post, don't break the seal, file it away carefully for some point in the future when it just might come in very, very handy for you.

There are other political issues and potential minefields surrounding the band. They involve boyfriends, girlfriends, mothers, fathers, husbands, and wives and even cheating amongst all, or some, of the above. For greater details on this I'd suggest you check out *The Ballad of Sean & Wilco*.

But not all the great stories about how badly it can all go wrong are fiction.

Let's take an example of say a group like Procol Harum. Now if there was ever a group who got it all wrong, and very badly wrong at that, it was Procol Harum.

Could I just say here that I, like a lot of people, was a major fan of this band's work, particularly their classic 'A Whiter Shade Of Pale' and I remember vividly the time they burst on the scene with one of *the* all-time great singles. But because of this amazing, perfect start to a career and the quality of that first song, I suppose, to be perfectly honest, I'd been expecting a lot more from them.

I remember that song stopping me dead in my tracks the first time I heard it. The combination of the classical quotes and the hint of blues forged a compelling backdrop to one of the most arresting and obscure set of lyrics ever penned. On top of which, of course, you had Gary Brooker's distinctive voice. Mr. Brooker surely is one of the most underrated soul singers the UK has ever produced.

The single was recorded in two takes, with no overdubs, and crashed straight into the charts at number 21 on May 25, 1967. The following week it was number four and then it took the coveted number one spot where it remained for six weeks before being toppled by The Beatles with 'All You Need Is Love'. 'A Whiter Shade Of Pale' hung around the charts for 15 weeks and was one of the biggest selling singles of the year. It was top of the charts in most of the countries that compiled charts, although for some strange reason it peaked at number five in America. I believe outside of The Beatles, it still remains one of the fastest selling singles ever released. It enjoyed another 10-week run in the UK charts during the summer of 1972 when it peaked at number

13. 'A Whiter Shade Of Pale' has reportedly sold in excess of 8 million copies worldwide.

To me, Procol Harum were the perfect band. They had a unique flower-power-cum-psychedelic look; they had an original sound, a very original, yet still pleasing, sound; a wonderful singer and, if 'A Whiter Shade Of Pale' was anything to go by, an original and classy in-built songwriting team in the form of lyricist Keith Reid and Gary Brooker, their singer and pianist.

I really was desperate to hear their first album – also entitled *Procol Harum* – and rushed out to buy it the day it was released. I suppose for the first clue to what lay ahead was a line on the album sleeve that proclaimed we should listen to the music, "in the spirit in which it was made." I'm not sure I've ever encountered such a disclaimer before or since. In 1967, albums were still novel enough to me that I knew every line on the sleeve, indeed I even seem to remember the intoxicating smell of the vinyl. Anyway, I took the album home and listened to it. And then I listened to it a bit more and then I found myself listening to it all weekend, hoping against hope that I would find the clue to unlock the secret of the sound of the creators of 'A Whiter Shade Of Pale'. I figured that anyone who had brought us such a masterpiece couldn't possibly have gotten it so wrong on their debut album and so the fault must be all mine.

So committed was I to their first monumental debut single I persevered with the album. But I always came up against their unappealing soundscape and their oppressive sound. It was like everyone, including the drummer, wanted desperately to be the lead instrument, so there was no foundation to hold the sound together. The result was an unsatisfactory, pretty much, all over the place kind of sound, which only occasionally allowed any hints of their potential to shine through. I faithfully bought their next album, *Shine On Brightly*, and their third, *A Salty Dog, and* their fourth, *Home*. Thankfully on all of them, particularly *A Salty Dog*, there were glimpses of the early genius but all in all you'd have to say it was an unrewarding and inaccessible body of work.

When I heard that first single, Procol Harum would have been the one group in the world I would never have earmarked as a one-hit-wonder band, but sadly with their follow-up, *Homburg*, peaking at number six and nothing much else since, but that's exactly the pile I've included them in for the past 30 years.

Then in 2000 Claes Johansen published a book he'd been working on for 17 years called, *Procol Harum – Beyond The Pale*.

From his book, I learned that Procol Harum had continuously suffered from managerial problems. At one point in their career, they seemed to be changing their management team at *least* once a week. Their record label was just in the process of being set up by their producer and they were changing distribution companies. Several band members didn't get on with each other and were fired even as 'A Whiter Shade Of Pale' was in the charts. Two ex-members of Gary Brooker's previous band, The Paramounts, replaced these band members. The Paramounts had split up following six flop singles and one EP so obviously that band hadn't been working either musically or personality-wise. So what I'm suggesting here is that there was already a bit of history there, maybe even a bit of intolerance between the musicians. What would have additionally fuelled the fires of discontent was the fact that the band members always felt that Procol Harum was really Gary Brooker and Keith Reid's band.

I also learnt that the band had taken only a week to record their all-important first album. On top of which, three different engineers were involved. That's always a very bad sign. It demonstrates that someone doesn't know what they're after so they're blaming others for their own inability to achieve their goals. The producer, as we've said, was most probably distracted continually with trying to set up his own label. From the outside, at least from the book, it didn't seem that the vital band spirit or band vibe was strong enough to carry the project through. It appears that the ex-Paramount members would have preferred to do other things, but they were persuaded to join Procol Harum only because the band, at least in name, had enjoyed the status of a Number One band.

There were opposing music factions in the band. Guitarist Robin Trower was trying to pull the band down the classic blues cum heavy guitar rock road. There was nothing wrong with that. Mr. Trower did enjoy considerable success in that direction later on with his own band, but it was obviously not a comfortable route for Procol Harum. Mathew Fisher obviously wanted them to be a Hammond Organ based band, while on the other hand, lyricist Keith Reid was desperately trying to emulate Dylan. In addition to which, Gary Brooker seemed confused about whether he wanted Procol Harum to be a Ray Charles' style of singer at the piano type of band, or a psychedelic band.

And as if that wasn't enough to contend with, managers, girlfriends, lyricists, record producers all had their own agendas, and what's more, they all seemed intent in pursuing them at the band's expense.

For example, when the first single entered at 21, neither manager nor agent was confident of the band's long-term potential, so they cashed in by immediately booking the band up for the following several months with £50 and £60 gigs (£750-ish in today's money). If they'd just held out for another two weeks, the band's fee would have been closer to £400 (£6,000-ish in today's money) but, more importantly they would have been able to have booked the band into a better class of gig, which they wouldn't have outgrown when the single reached the top of the charts.

This indeed proved to be the case and so all the gigs had to be pulled, cancelled.

Please note here that agents, not *all* agents I hasten to add, hate to cancel gigs. It's a minimum of twice the work for no income. So, when you need to cancel, it's usually a decision you or your manager need to take.

The pulling of those gigs would certainly have done Procol Harum's reputation a considerable amount of damage. You see, those who buy tickets and albums don't really know or care about managers, agents, concert promoters, record companies, record producers, and what all of the above may, or may not, be up to behind the scenes. So when an artist cancels shows, the fans don't blame the managers, the agents or the promoters. When the artist releases an inferior album, the fans don't blame the manager, the record producer or the record company. In both instances the fans blame the artist and nine times out of 10 the fans will go off and find someone else to be a fan to. And goodness knows there are enough great artists out there all vying for their attention.

So, in my humble opinion, poor Procol Harum never stood a chance. It now appears that with all of the behind-the-scenes turmoil going on, they got off to a terrible start. So bad a start in fact it was always going to be impossible for them to realise their full potential.

Okay, let's ask the hypothetical question, "How could a band like Procol Harum have got it right?"

Well, I suppose the most obvious goal would have been to ensure that their team of musicians, manager, agent, record company, record producer were all on the same page. They should have tried to resolve all of their musical differences before they launched the band. Sure the single was number one and that did put a certain amount of pressure on those involved to deliver, and to deliver quickly, but they should have also considered the fact that the initial success would give them a certain amount of freedom and time to get it right.

They *should* have waited until they created what they considered to be their perfect debut album. If only to match their perfect debut single. Once you put your music out there, it's out there for eternity. They certainly had the material for a great debut album – a point proved when material written at the same time as 'A Whiter Shade Of Pale' appeared on (much) later albums – and they certainly had an amazing vocalist so, on paper at least, all they needed was a worthy producer. Somewhere in the midst of their records is a unique sound trying desperately hard to break through. At times they get so close that the glimpses you are permitted to see and hear are quite amazing. 'A Whiter Shade Of Pale' was, as we have already said, recorded in two takes with no overdubs, which proves, to me at least, that there was a naturalness present. All they needed was to work out what exactly their musical goals were, and find the right person to help them achieve those goals. Can you imagine how the band would have sounded if they'd worked with George Martin?

Yes, George Martin had a classical background. Yes, he was a studio visionary – check the production of *Sgt. Pepper's* and the equipment available at the time if you need convincing. But he also had a sense of humour and it was his ability to combine all three qualities that made his productions as successful as they were. All great music should have at least a hint of humour. In Procol Harum's production, it's disastrously missing. Sure there's hints of humour in the lyrics and some of the music, but that's never allowed to come through in the production.

When an artist, any artist, is enjoying creative or commercial success and they are comfortable in their environment, that's exactly the time, with the confidence high, that their creative juices are flowing and they are capable of being inspired to greater heights. Procol Harum didn't ever get to the stage where they could enjoy the luxury of that cocoon. If they had, can you imagine what they could have achieved creatively?

With Procol Harum, I believe with a passion that they *really* were, in the words of the proverbial fisherman, "the big one that got away". Unlike the fisherman's dream though, Procol Harum passed so close, anyone who wanted to, could almost have touched them.

This is certainly not meant to be a criticism of the band. I mention them primarily because they were potentially brilliant and could have been so big if only they'd taken the time to get it right.

So, in short, Procol Harum is an extremely frustrating example of what happens when you don't get all your stuff together properly.

★

It's also important to remember that for this *playing live* circuit to continue, we depend on teenagers sitting in their houses – all the way from Aberdeen to Anglesey and Magherafelt to Middlesborough – looking at an artist appearing on television and being inspired by them to pick up a guitar and attempt to write and perform songs. It doesn't matter if the artists they view are Jackson Browne, Bob Dylan, Coldplay or The Be Good Tanyas. All that matters is that TV and radio provide an outlet for quality music; it doesn't matter the type, as long as it's good.

My worry is that if these potential artists are only subjected to programmes like the Brits, then all they'll be encouraged to do is vomit.

That annual gross spectacle has nothing whatsoever to do with any of the section of the music business I've been talking about over these pages. It's very important that new artists realise that the Brits is nothing more than an annual marketing exercise and opportunity for the British record companies. It very rarely represents the best of UK talent. Please do not feel that this shite is the best of anything, let alone the best of British music.

Of course the basic premise is flaky. How can Pulp possibly be better than Blur. Yes, you can say they are and give them an award but that doesn't necessarily make it true. It's the same as saying a Jaguar S Type is better than a Massey Ferguson Tractor. What they *could* say is that Blur is more popular than Pulp because they sell more records. But if we go down that route, we're always going to end up with The Beatles, because they sold more records than anyone ever did or probably ever will.

It's very important to realise that the record companies probably dish out the awards to those who are prepared to show up, or to those who are a record company's current pet project. These are the exact same record companies who organise the event in the first place.

Occasionally, by the law of averages, they do get it right *sometimes*, but the other 95% of the time they are not even close, so it's important for our would-be artists in general and Goggles Anonymous in particular not to be disheartened and, if anything, take heart from your exclusion.

Before you worry about whether or not your material is worthy of these companies, please take comfort in the fact that I guarantee you that if you ever have occasion to trawl through the disregarded demos of any record company, you'll find the demo tapes of the majority of great artists who subsequently found success with another record company. I tell you this only because *they* don't know, *we* don't know, *nobody* knows really, except you, and it is *your* confidence in what you are doing and what you *have* to do that will see you through this to the other side.

It's my view that artists like The Beatles, Dylan, Ray Davies, Pink Floyd, Genesis and Coldplay, any successful artists really – no matter how unlikely their chances may have seemed in their formative years – were always going to make it. That's something that Goggles Anonymous can take solace in, or not.

But before you start to think, "God if there was a chance those class acts could not have made it with those great songs and those incredible voices, then what chance do I have?" Or "Goodness, do I really want to bother with the music business at all?" let's start to think and discuss your agent.

Around this time, Goggles Anonymous will probably have gone as far as it's possible to go without an agent.

My advice to all new artists is that the first person you need to employ is your agent.

4

THE AGENT

Agents do everything, and they do everything because they have to. Most of the time, when we take on a new act, it's too early for a manager to be involved. Apart from anything else, artists need to get gigs before they can get the attention of managers or record companies, so the agent is the obvious starting point. Then as an agent of your new fledgling act, you have either to help out or watch your new hopefuls go down the pan.

A good agent will be pivotal in your career. Not only will an agent (hopefully) fulfil the old-fashioned role of an agent, i.e. secure live appearances – gigs – for you, but they will also help set you up with managers, publishers, lawyers and record companies. They will also relay to you:

THE 10 GOLDEN RULES FOR GIGGING MUSICIANS

1. Always arrive on time.
2. Ensure all your gear works properly in advance.
3. Keep punctual stage times.
4. Look good. There is a vast difference between dressing up or down to suit a fashion and dressing scruffily.
5. Have a well-rehearsed set. It really does not matter what style of music you choose to play, it matters only that you play it well.
6. Be polite to everyone you come into contact with. Apart from anything else, it makes your life a lot easier.
7. Always have plenty of printed promotional material (photos, biographies and posters) available.
8. Always collect your fee before you leave the building.
9. Never slag off your barber's football team.
10. Have fun!

Now if you follow these basic rules it won't necessarily mean you will be successful – that depends entirely on how people react to your music – but it does mean you are going to be noticed, and it does mean you're not going to miss opportunities. In other words, at least you'll have a fair chance.

FINDING AN AGENT

So, how do you find your agent?

I've included a list of some of the London Agencies in the appendix. But you know what? Do you know who the best agent is for your act? It's quite simply the agent who likes your act most. The agent who genuinely gets what you're doing. Don't you see, when that agent comes to sell your act to a club or a promoter, if he has genuine enthusiasm, this enthusiasm will (hopefully) be infectious? A lot of people, even people already in the music business, feel that if they get a big agent, or a big manager, they've got it made.

Wrong!

There are no such things as big managers or big agents. There are, however, agents and managers who represent BIG artists and that's an entirely different matter.

Look through the list and see if you, or any of your friends, recognise any of the names.

I mean, does anyone in your immediate circle know anyone in one of the agencies? You know, know them well enough that they could ring them up and put a word in the agent's ear to watch out for your demo tape or, even better, to try and get the agent down to see you next time you perform. Same as before, you want to find a way of getting their attention, to lift your name up out of the pile of other artists submitting their music. You need to do something to grab their attention, to ensure they seek out your cassette or CD and listen to it with open ears.

I remember an artist, Brendan Crocker was his name – it still is in fact – and he sent us a few demos, which we hadn't picked up on. He was a nice enough guy and all, but he felt he wasn't getting anywhere with us. Anyway, he was a friend of Andy Kershaw, whom we knew very well as being the Leeds University Social Secretary (later to become a roadie for Billy Bragg and then to become one of the BBC's best DJs). Brendan had Andy fix up a meeting with us and he came into the office with his guitar and a bottle of whiskey and he sat the bottle of whiskey on my desk and said: "There you are, good buddy, that's a little present for you." Then he took his guitar out of its case and continued, "and now I'd like to play you a few tunes."

I'm not a whiskey drinker but I admired his (other) bottle. I was in awe of the fact that he had the guts to sing his songs across my desk. That had never happened before. In the good old days, a proper agent would have had an upright piano in his office so artists could perform personal auditions. I always visualise the great agents sitting down at the piano, resting a cigar on the edge of the keyboard and saying to the artist, in their best Tito Burns accent, "Okay, you hum it and I'll play it." For the true Tito Burns accent, check out the agent in Dylan's groundbreaking documentary, *Don't Look Back*.

Anyway, getting back to Brendan Crocker. I liked his voice and (when I eventually got to hear them) I loved his band, The Five O'clock Shadows. We signed them because Brendan had made his band and his music stand out from all the rest of the stuff we were receiving daily.

Obviously not everyone can do it that way, if only due to the fact that the agent would never find time to be on the phone looking after the interests of his signed artists.

Talking about demos (demonstration tapes/compact discs), the best demos to send to prospective music business companies should contain four tracks – your best four tracks. Less is more. If they like your initial four songs, there will be lots of other occasions for them to hear the remainder of your material. Spend all your money on four tracks. Remember this is not meant to be the definitive final recorded version – all you are trying to do is to demonstrate the song to a degree that the listener can hear its potential. It's not advisable to send live recordings initially. Like the music, keep your cassette (or CD) jacket simple, the name of your group, the names of the songs, the name(s) of the song-writer(s) and a telephone number. There is no need to send a large letter describing how the mix isn't the way you like it to be. If you don't like it, don't send it to anyone. If you don't like it, throw it in the dustbin. Only send in things you absolutely love. I still get cassettes and CDs sent in with wee notes saying, the new stuff, which will be on the *next* demo, is much better. Thank you very much, but I'd prefer to wait and hear the better stuff.

If the agent likes what he hears, he'll either drop you a line, or ring you up for a chat. He's looking to *check* you *out*, maybe he'll come to a gig and see what you're like live, or maybe his call will be to check if you have any other demos. Now the other **equally** important thing at this point is for you to use this time to *check* him and his office out. Too many artists are so happy that someone, anyone, is paying attention and praising their music that they will sign anything with anyone who comes along. I've had artists come in to see me who are so desperate to "get a deal with a London agency" that they will literally do *any* deal, sign *anything* just to get started. Not a good idea for either agent or artist. No matter what deal an artist is prepared to sign with an agent at the beginning of their career, they will start to resent the agent later in their career if they discover the agent took advantage and the deal was not a fair one. No matter what papers or contracts the artist has signed with an agent, it won't matter a fig, quite simply they are going to want to move. Artists, when they discover they have been taken advantage of business-wise, are as single-minded in their pursuit of vengeance as those wronged in matters of the heart.

This will hopefully explain to you why some of the artist disputes you read about in the papers are so ugly, aggressive and frequently, to those on the outside, quite illogical. When artists realise that they've been ripped off they don't want to redress the balance and negotiate a new, fairer deal. No, they want to get even with the SOAB who has been ripping them off.

Sadly, many artists allow these initial bickerings to prejudice their dealings with the music industry for the remainder of their career. Chuck Berry, for instance, is legendary for his dealings. His rider quite clearly calls for a certain type of Fender Twin amplifier and if he arrives at the venue and an inferior model of Fender amplifier has been supplied, well, it's not even that he's an unhappy man and throws a wobbler. No, he's quite charming. He advises the promoter that he will perform using the inferior equipment, but to do so will cause him mental distress and to subject himself to this mental distress he is going to have to be compensated. I don't know how much it is these days, but when I did a couple of shows with him in Ireland a few years ago it was $1,000. Mr. Berry's contract also stipulates that he will perform for 50 minutes. He fulfils this commitment, literally to the second, leaving the audience going totally ape. If the promoter wants to protect the venue furniture he will go and try to coax Mr. Berry to do an encore. Mr. Berry is generally happy to oblige. Naturally, as it's outside the duration of the original contract there's a premium to pay, in the neighbourhood of $500. And he's quite within his rights. But perhaps if he'd been treated better earlier in his career . . .

Fair is always fair and will last a long time.

As with your manager, you could and should have a long relationship with your agent. Chopping and changing offices sends out a certain message. So it helps, big time, if you actually like your agent. Get to know the agent, let him get to know you. In your agent you don't just need someone who can get you gigs, that's very short-sighted. To have a chance of succeeding and successfully launching your concert career you need an agent who has a vision.

I mean, I realise that this may all sound a wee bit obvious but you'd be surprised how many potentially great artists never got off the starting blocks just because their agent didn't have the foresight for the next several moves, let alone know how to plan them.

A good agent will help you by-pass all the time wasters. They'll know managers, record companies, music publishers, solicitors and accountants. They're perfectly placed to help you put your team together.

If you've already got a mate who you trust and you want to be your manager because you both have a shared vision – even though the manager doesn't have the experience – then that's all the more reason to secure a great agent; someone who can help both of you through this minefield.

For now though we're talking about agents. Let's not worry too much about managers at the minute; we'll deal with them in greater detail later. On the agency front, the next subject that is going to rear its ugly head is contracts.

Should you sign a contract? Well, I suppose the honest answer to that is, if you can get away without signing one, then you should try and do that. The problem is, any agent worth his salt will not lift a telephone on your behalf until you've signed on the dotted line. There are a few reasons for that and I'll go into them here in the hope that it will help you make your decision, particularly if you ever come knocking on Asgard's door.

In the perfect world, everyone is honourable and once you agree to work together and agree *fair* terms, that should be more than enough. Unfortunately the reality is different. Why? Because artists want to keep their options open, to see how good the agent is; or they are hoping eventually to find an agent who will be cheaper; maybe even they are hoping to find a manager and they know that manager may have his own favourite agent. Again, there are variations on the theme.

From the agent's perspective the reason any agents worth their salt will require you to sign a contract is because they're going to want to protect their investment and their reputation. No matter how successful an artist is, they will run at a loss for the agency for at least the first year. In that year, hopefully, the agency will exploit its relationship with promoters on your behalf. The last thing the agent needs is for the act to then run off to another agency and consequently (possibly) another set of promoters. Another reason why an agent should want to protect themselves with a signed contract is because there is a chance the artist might find a manager. There is a good chance this manager will have his own connections, for instance his own favourite agents, who he'd prefer to work with. And the last reason is that there is always an agent out there who will represent an artist for a lesser commission. So I'm afraid all good agents should want you to sign on the dotted line.

What's an agent's contract like? Well, most of the agency contracts I have seen are a pile of rubbish. They ramble on and on for three or four pages and are very biased on the agent's side. At Asgard we have a simple, single page letter of agreement, to wit:

1. The essence of the agreement: Representation for live work.
2. The period covered: Four years.
3. The commission payable: 15% of gross fees.
4. The territory covered: The World.

So, right from the start, everyone knows exactly what they are getting into, and there are no excuses acceptable down the line. Once you are up and running and start to achieve reasonable fees, most agents are prepared to renegotiate their commission rate down to 10%. This is, of course, for everywhere except North America and Canada, where your UK agent will have to pay an American sub-agent out of his, or her, 15%.

I would say, if I were a manager responsible for signing my artist to an agent, I would ask for a **key-man-clause** in my artist's contract. Effectively, what this means is, should my artist's agent ever move to another agency, my act wouldn't be stuck for the remainder of the contractual period with an office who, although not interested in my act any more, are not honourable enough to let my act go.

It doesn't matter how big an agency is, or how great their reputation is, unless there is someone in the office who really cares about you and your music, you are not going to have a fair chance of success. This applies particularly if you go the Star Manager route. The Star Manager will ensure the agency of their main act will sign you. The agency will be happy to sign you, if only to keep Star Manager happy; it doesn't however mean that the agency will get you enough, or even any, gigs and they will have a list as long as both arms of justifiable excuses for not getting you gigs.

So my advice is, don't sign with an office, sign with an agent.

Finding artists is as difficult for an agent as finding agents is for an artist. Every time an agent goes to hear a new group, in order to be able to continue to do their job properly, the agent has to think that there is a chance the artist in question could quite possibly be going to be the next Beatles. Mind you, not that The Beatles were ever the new anything. But they were a great live act, way before they wrote great songs or made great records.

Equally, for this to really work, the group the agent goes to hear have to believe the same thing and be totally committed to what they are doing.

*

For my own part, I became an agent by accident. I had no great design or master plan. As I mentioned earlier, when I started I was simply helping a bunch of mates get up on stage and play their music. The Beatles came along and turned me – and most of the rest of the world – on and I moved to London thinking that's where the music scene was, so that was where I wanted to be.

London in 1967 was a hoot. I had a chance to see and hear first hand the artists I'd been reading about in *NME* for the previous couple of years. I had no sooner unpacked my bags than I was growing a moustache and making my first pilgrimage to the Marquee Club in the West End. It seemed to me that there were clubs on every street corner where you could hear music. *Sgt. Pepper's Lonely Hearts Club Band* was the number one album on the charts – it held the top position from June 3 until October 14 – and flower power was in full flow. Tie-dye shirts, granddad shirts, loon pants, Fair Isle sweaters, corduroy shoes, National Health wire framed glasses were the order of the day. Everything was loud and colourful. Kaftans were very cool. I remember buying one but not being able to pluck up the courage to wear it. I grew up in a community where people would have said, "Who let you out dressed like that?" and it takes a lifetime to outgrow that. People in the music business still went to work dressed in suits, shirts and ties – there was still the (very) odd gentleman wandering about with bowler hat and brolly – but the lunatics were gradually, and very successfully, taking over the asylum. The other albums in the charts at that point included: *The Sound*

Of Music, Scott by Scott Walker, *Best Of The Beach Boys, Dr. Zhivago, Fiddler On The Roof, Buddy Holly's Greatest Hits* and albums by Tom Jones, The Jimi Hendrix Experience, Englebert Humperdinck and John Mayall's Bluesbreakers. The singles chart from September of that year (1967) probably shows better what was starting to happen musically. We had The Small Faces singing about their 'Itchycoo Park', The Rolling Stones wishing they were The Beatles with 'We Love You', Keith West's 'Excerpt From A Teenage Opera' (did he ever release the full Opera?), Flowerpot Men giving an early nod to flower power with 'Let's Go To San Francisco', The Beach Boys' 'Heroes And Villains', and The Move with 'Flowers In The Rain' (the first ever record to be played on the newly formed Radio One). The Kinks were between two absolute classics, 'Waterloo Sunset' and 'Autumn Almanac'; Traffic's seminal 'Hole In My Shoe' was peaking; you had 'Reflections' from The Supremes and chirpy Cliff was holding up the old guard with 'The Day I Met Marie', the 42nd of his 125, and still counting, hits. Radio One was formed at the Government's pleasure. Actually, they ordered the BBC to come up with something as an alternative to the recently banned, but very healthy, Pirate Radio stations.

When I moved to London first, I didn't necessarily want to work in the music business. I didn't know how you would go about doing that. There were no exams you could take, nor were there any qualifications that would gain you access on the fast track to *Ready Steady Go!*

Fortunately for me I was in London at the same time a few of the Irish artists were starting to do well in England. We're talking about artists like Taste, Skid Row, Grannies Intentions and Thin Lizzy. I was invited to cover their progress for a Belfast newspaper called *Cityweek*. Infrequent articles grew into a weekly column.

Taste were an amazing group. I just positively lived to go and see and hear them absolutely everywhere they played from the Marquee Club to the Toby Jug. I'd follow them all over London, never being able to hear enough of them. Taste comprised Rory Gallagher, lead guitar and vocals, Charlie McCracken on bass guitar and John "Wilsie" Wilson on drums. Rory was a very gifted musician and one of the most natural performers I have ever witnessed. The minute he walked on stage and plugged his guitar into his battered Vox AC30, he metamorphosed from this polite Donegal gentleman into this manic but masterful giant of a performer. But with Rory, it wasn't like it was an act in the way you feel it might just be an act with someone like say Bruce Springsteen. Don't get me wrong, Bruce is also amazing live, but Rory, well the minute he plugged his guitar in, it was like he was also plugging himself into some central energy-generating force. Every single note he played hit you smack between the eyes. He'd chase the note the whole way around the stage until he captured it, played around with it for a while before throwing it to the audience. He turned an audience on in a way I have never witnessed anyone else do. Going to his performances was a *total* experience; you would leave ecstatic, but totally drained.

And off stage he'd always be a gent and have a few words for the folks back home via my newspaper column. Later, I was privileged to have been his agent for a few years, by which time he'd long since disbanded Taste and was working under his own name. But he never ceased to amaze me as a performer. You know what? He was the perfect artist for an agent to represent. With Rory, you didn't have to depend on hit records, singles on the radio, television appearances, press or whatever. No, he was a one-man promotional phenomenon. All you needed to do was to get him on a stage, any stage, and he'd do the rest. He made a real connection with the people who came to see him, they became his fans, and then, as part of the word-of-mouth process, which always was, and always will be, the single most effective promotional tool, they spread the word. Rory Gallagher was the real McCoy and goodness knows there are few of those around.

Anyway, I was happily writing away about Taste, Skid Row and Van Morrison and then a mate of mine, the guitarist from The Blues By Five, formed a group called Fruupp and he wanted to bring them straight to London, so he asked me if I'd get him a couple of gigs in London so they could get over here and find a manager and a record deal, then live happily ever after. Five years, four albums and a thousand gigs later, they still hadn't found a manager and, by default, I found myself their manager . . . along with being their agent, roadie, sound engineer and lyricist – basically they couldn't afford anyone else. In those days, the Seventies, record companies didn't throw large advances at groups – well at least they didn't throw a large one at us – so we lived hand to mouth from the proceeds of the gigs. The main spin-off for me, although I didn't realise it at the time, was that I was gaining first-hand experience of all the venues around Europe. I'd meet, and look in the eye, most of the promoters on the circuit, which I suppose gave me the best experience necessary for being an agent. On top of which, I'd found something I really enjoyed doing.

Becoming an agent is one thing, finding your first act is slightly more complicated. As an agent, the only thing you have is your reputation and your reputation is based to some degree on the acts that you represent. As we've discussed, some acts only want to sign with an agent they consider to be a big agent.

Conversely, if you, as an agent, have no artists, it's very difficult to entice artists to sign with you.

Fruupp split up on a tidal wave of indifference, so there I was, an agent without any artists. Eventually I did manage to persuade a group to work with me. It was The George Hatcher Band (affectionately known as The Margaret Thatcher Band in the Dryden Chambers) and we found them lots of gigs and then a few more gigs and the chap at George Hatcher's record company – Andrew Laurder – noticed that we were getting George lots of gigs and he'd just signed a new band and he thought maybe we could do the same job for his new group. They were called The Buzzcocks, and we did manage to fill their date sheet over the next few years when they enjoyed eight chart singles, one chart EP and three chart albums. It was just as well they'd all that success to celebrate, because they certainly liked their champagne did The Buzzcocks. Because we had The Buzzcocks, The Undertones were receptive to our advances and then Penetration, Human League, The Gang Of 4, The Lurkers all followed shortly thereafter.

And the point in telling you this is that it's that easy, or that hard, to become an agent.

Sometimes finding an artist is one thing, working with them is something else. I remember being very excited at taking on Clifford T Ward for agency representation. *Home Thoughts From Abroad* is a wonderful album full of beautiful and imaginative songs. I found Clifford to be a very nice man but so painfully, painfully shy that in the several years I represented him he never once ventured onto a concert stage.

From an agent's point of view, artists fall into two main categories, the first is new artists, who you are continuously looking for, and the second are the established artists whose music you love. I'd been a major fan of Jackson Browne, Nick Lowe, The Blue Nile, Van Morrison, Rory Gallagher, Tom Waits and Ray Davies before I got a chance to work with them.

In fact I remember, back in Ulster, hitching up to The Embassy Ballroom in Derry to try and meet the manager and blag a booking for Blues By Five. The manager was in the ballroom routining GoGo dancers. The piece of music he was using for the girls to do their routine to was 'Waterloo Sunset' by The Kinks. I'd already thought that particular single was a classic, but 30 plays (that same day) later, I was convinced it was the work of a genius. So you can imagine how thrilled I was 25 years later when I meet and work with the songwriter in question, Mr. Ray Davies, and his band, The Kinks. Ray Davies is one of those cabbie friendly names. Do you know what I mean? Okay, you're sitting in the back of a cab and the cabbie knows that if he can make a connection with you, he has a chance of getting a (bigger) tip. So he says:

"What do you do for a living Guv?"

"I'm an agent in the music business."

"And what exactly does an agent in the music business do?"

"I find work for several artists."

"Oh, right. And who do you represent?'

Now if you say the Penguin Café Orchestra, whom I did represent and I love dearly, he's likely to say:

"Really, that must be interesting for you."

Or if he listens to Classic FM maybe he'll say authoritatively:

"And who's the conductor?"

However, if you answer his original question with, "Ray Davies", he'll immediately break into a smile and say something like.: "Oh yeah, and isn't he just the best songwriter England has ever produced. I picked him up once in my cab and isn't he just the nicest person you'll ever meet."

Both facts are, in my humble opinion, true, and it's also kinda remarkable that Ray Davies seems to have travelled in every single London cab, well at least the ones I've been in, that is.

It's funny, but not a coincidence I feel, that two of the most professional artists I've worked with came out of Sixties groups, Ray Davies of The Kinks and Van Morrison of Them. Although the Sixties pop group boom marked the beginning of the end of the old school of entertainers, some of the old school's good qualities seem to have rubbed off on the, then, new wave. Someone certainly had instilled the show-must-go-on attitude in the children of the Sixties. Actually, I suppose if they were all in pop groups in the Sixties, it probably means that they were children of the Forties and Fifties. But you see, in all of this, you, the artist, don't sell your tickets and your records and your t-shirts by accident. I know I've said that before, and it's so important I might even say it again. It is a business and the core business has to be taken care of.

WIN YOURSELF A REPUTATION BY PUTTING ON A PROFESSIONAL SHOW

Eight tips to help achieve this reputation:

> Always tour with a top quality sound system.
> Use classy, but never overbearing lights.
> Look good.
> Appear on stage punctually.
> Graciously play your hit/hits.★
> Play a full set.
> Meet and sign autographs for your fans.
> Be careful when you cross the road.

(★ delete as appropriate)

When you've won this reputation, then your audience will stay with you forever and I do mean forever – Cliff Richard sells as many tickets today as he puts on sale, and that's a hell of a lot more tickets than he was selling in the Fifties and Sixties. Jackson Browne works to packed houses continuously, year in year out; same for Ray Davies, and I've seen very few artists who consistently send the crowd home with smiles on their faces the way Ray Davies does. Bob Dylan still plays a staggering 150 concerts per year, all over the world, all of which sell out.

The live career of other seemingly more popular artists depends very much on whether or not they have a single in the charts. If they have, they're fine; if they haven't it's a very hard slog. It's not that the record buying audience turn off from the artists; it's more that the radio does, and if you're not on the radio, no matter who you are, it's pretty impossible for your audience to be aware of your current music.

If you intend to forge a career making and performing music, all your early moves and decisions are vitally important and professionalism is the key.

I mean, of course, that professionalism is the key *assuming* you've got the songs to which people will react.

We were talking about how an agent finds an act, weren't we? There is no singular way. Take Van Morrison for instance. I got my break with him just because I was one of his fans, had been since the Them days. We (Asgard) used to do a lot of shows in Ireland and Van had taken on Harvey Goldsmith, as his new UK manager. Plans were afoot for him to return from America for a tour, this would have been around the time of the *Wavelength* album. We'd been negotiating with the UK

Management for ages about presenting Van in his homeland. We'd set up two shows in Belfast, three in Dublin and one in Cork. Then we received the news that the UK based manager was no longer the manager. Through the record company, we found that Van had appointed a new American manager so we got in touch with them and tried to continue the talks. We were advised it would be impossible for Van to come over just to play Ireland.

"Okay, we'll do the UK for him as well," I said, gulping large dollops of air as we'd never promoted a UK tour before.

"Okay, then make us an offer," they said.

They further advised us that they would have to entertain offers from several UK promoters. Now every single person I knew had a copy of *Astral Weeks* – that might have said more about my friends than the popularity of the music, but I didn't think so. I also had a few mates who worked in record stores (mainly Musicland in Berwick Street) and they had told me that *Astral Weeks* had been their BIGGEST selling import album ever. So we made our offer for Van to play three nights at Hammersmith Odeon (3,400 tickets per night) while our competitors were offering The Venue (one of Richard Branson's early properties, a stone's throw from Victoria station, and now closed. It only had a 640 capacity).

So we got the tour, which included the original six shows in Ireland, three in London and another dozen or so shows around the UK. The *entire* tour sold out the first day it went on sale and, for me, it was the beginning of an eight-year working relationship with Van Morrison. That first tour I worked on finished in Newcastle and the tour bus returned to London immediately after the concert. En route from New-castle Van walked up and down the aisle of the bus strumming his guitar and singing Beatle songs, Beach Boys songs, Hank Williams songs, country classics. He even took requests and knew the chords and lyrics of every song thrown at him. All in all it was a unique and enormously enjoyable experience for all those on board. Yes, Van Morrison, acting as a human jukebox on the return journey from Newcastle is my over-riding memory of that tour.

Now, because we represented Mr. Morrison, when we made our overtures to other artists the doors opened a bit more easily. I'd been a fan of Jackson Browne since his very first album. I loved his voice and I loved his songwriting even more. He made records which for me were just perfect. I'd been to see him live a few times and played his album *For Everyman* every waking hour God sent. His record company had brought him over to England once, but from what I could gather, he didn't have an agent, so I started to track him down. His manager would have polite conversations with me, but the crux of the matter was that he was becoming mega in America and there was more than enough work for him to do there. I politely pushed on, advising them that, with a few well-planned tours, he could be mega this side of the Atlantic too. Then I did the Van Morrison tour and someone in Van's camp (the tour manager) knew someone in Jackson's camp, so the next time I rang they were more receptive. Five months later, Jackson Browne was on a seven-week tour of Europe. Can you imagine being able to hear one of your favourite artists live every night (well excluding nights off, of course) for seven weeks?

One of the partners in Jackson Browne's management company turned out to be one of the managers of Crosby, Stills & Nash, and Jackson Browne is a very good friend of Graham Nash. Within a year of the Jackson Browne tour, we were touring Crosby, Stills & Nash around Europe. Sadly Mr. Crosby was still a bit of a casualty in those days. Not, I hasten to add, during the time he was on stage; for that hour and a half every night he sang as sweetly as a bird, but it was depressing to see (up close) how effectively chemicals can wreck a life. Thankfully, all his friends rallied round him and by the next time they toured Europe, he was a different person, different in that when you looked into his eyes you could see someone looking back at you.

At Asgard over the years we've been lucky enough to work with some of the world's greatest blues artists. I'm talking about people like John Lee Hooker, Buddy Guy, Taj Mahal, Robert Cray and Sonny Terry & Brownie McGee.

We represented Sonny Terry & Brownie McGee towards the end of their career together. I remember my first very bizarre meeting with them. Although I'd been through all the tour details in advance with their American representative in NYC, the artists insisted on meeting with me at their hotel the minute they arrived in London. I sat down with them. Sonny was probably the best blues harp player who ever lived and was a big, gentle, warm, smiling man and Brownie I always felt was somewhat underrated as a blues artist. Maybe he too felt that to be the case, because he was always a little guarded, withdrawn even. Anyway, I sat down with them and, as requested, went through the tour details with them. The cities, the venues and of course the fees and the state of the deposits. All artists are keen to ensure that 50% of their fees have been deposited with their agent before stepping on stage for their first concert.

Brownie asked me a few questions as we went along, and then, just when I thought we'd covered everything, Sonny asked me the same questions all over again and had me repeat the fees. You see, by the time I met them, they hadn't actually spoken to each other for about 17 years. So I found it quite funny that, although they would never allow any meetings to take place unless they were both in attendance, they insisted that you address them both separately and directly. It didn't matter that they both had to hear the information twice; it was only important that you addressed each of them as individuals.

I still find it quite incredible that two artists could work together, never communicate with each other for 17 years, but still gel so brilliantly on stage. As I mentioned, the shows we did with them were at the end of their career, but I was dumbstruck by the power they generated nightly on stage.

Another quick example of how an agent finds an act. I first encountered Tanita Tikaram playing in the acoustic room at the Mean Fiddler. I represented an artist, Paul Brady, who was playing a week at the main room of the Fiddler when it was in Harlesden. While awaiting Mr. Brady's performance I escaped the packed, thirsty room by retreating to the more sedate acoustic room for a quiet cup of tea. It was an open microphone night in the acoustic room. During such evenings about six acts would turn up, some with friends in tow, in the hope that their 20 minutes on stage might lead to something more. The thing that pulled me into Tanita's music initially was not her songs but her stagecraft. During her second song, the people at the table closest to the stage started to rabbit on a bit. As Tanita's performance progressed, I could see that she was growing increasingly annoyed with their rude behaviour. And how did she choose to deal with the potentially ugly situation? Throwing a strop? No way. Eventually she stopped singing, but continued to play her guitar. The offending table, oblivious to what was happening on stage, continued laughing and guffawing. Tanita, still playing her guitar, wandered over to their side of the stage and started to glare at them. Eventually, one by one, they became aware of this presence on stage glaring at them and they grew self-conscious and stopped talking. When they were all silent Tanita simply strolled back to the centre stage microphone and picked up her song again. I thought it was amazing how she dealt with that potential show- wrecking scene with such a cool reaction. She immediately grabbed my attention and I tuned in completely to the remainder of her set with even greater interest. I remember wondering how someone who looked so young could act with such a seasoned professionalism. To top that I learned afterwards it was her very first public performance.

I was at the venue that night as an agent and ended up becoming her manager.

A similar episode helped Dire Straits find a manager. Ed Bicknell was brought along to Dingwalls Dancehall with a view to becoming their agent. The minute the band struck up, Ed was so magnetised by the vision of the guitar Mark Knopfler was playing, he immediately turned to the record company representative and said, "I'd really like to manage these guys." At the time he didn't really know what being a manager entailed but that guitar was all it took for Ed to want to buy into the dream.

Later, when Ed was their manager, he admitted to Mark that it hadn't exactly been the band's music that had attracted him. He conceded it was the classic vibrant Stratocaster that caught his eye.

"Well, it had to be red, didn't it?" Mark admitted, when he discovered Ed was as big a fan of Hank Marvin as he was.

The most famous case of how a manager and group met? Probably everyone in the world knows that Brian Epstein came to work with The Beatles as a result of a young man, Raymond Jones, coming into his record shop requesting a record by a local group. There's hardly a day that goes by that I don't enjoy the music that resulted from that particular partnership.

Tom Waits is another artist I'm a big fan of and I had tried on several occasions in the Seventies and Eighties to represent him as an agent. I'd just be starting to develop a relationship with a manager when they would become the ex-manager. Every time I visited Los Angeles I would meet with someone or other about the possibility of representing Tom Waits. As I mentioned, this went on for years, and in one such year I was in America doing the rounds and had ended up in Los Angeles. As in the early days with the ballroom owners, I discovered nothing beats the in-person approach. A face-to-face meeting with an American manager or artist is worth about two-dozen faxes or phone calls. As ever, when I found myself with time to kill between meetings, I'd head off to Tower Records on Sunset Boulevard for a good old browse through the racks. The minute I entered the vibrant record store I spied all the promotional material for *One From The Heart*, which was a soundtrack album Tom Waits and Crystal Gayle had just released.

I'd already seen the movie and loved the music, so I immediately asked one of the assistants for a copy of the album.

"Oh, we're very sorry, sir, we've sold out of that particular album," the shop assistant replied. She dropped to a conspiratorial whisper as she continued, "in fact, I just sold our last copy to Tom Waits himself and he's standing . . . don't look now . . . just behind you."

She smiled awkwardly, gesturing with her eyes and nose to my left.

I browsed casually in his direction and when I was close enough to make eye contact, I introduced myself. "Hi I'm Paul Charles from Asgard in London and I've been trying to work with you for several years."

Sometimes you've got one shot and one shot only and you have to make your pitch simply and quickly. Tom and his wife Kathleen had heard of my efforts and were very friendly. We retreated to a nearby cafe for a cup of tea and a chat. An hour or so later I was their agent.

The first tour I did with Tom Waits was a treat, a real treat in every sense of the word. With Tom Waits you not only get to book the show and hear magic music every night, you also get to help put the show together and help stage it nightly. My additional duties were to make *rain* fall on the stage every night at the appropriate time and to figure out how to make a bright light shine on Tom's face from inside his raggedy top hat. The former we perfected on the third night of the tour, using a cardboard box filled with small pieces of polythene set up in the lighting rig and attached to a piece of string, the other end of which was in my hand. The latter challenge, producing the beam of white light from the top hat, took until the very last concert to master, but master it we did.

The Blue Nile, John Lee Hooker, Roy Orbison, Paul Brady, Christy Moore, Mary Black, Rory Gallagher, Gerry Rafferty, John Prine, John Sebastion and Nick Lowe were all artists whose music I loved before I had a chance to work with them. I suppose the point I'd like to make is that I don't rave about them because I'm lucky enough to work with them; it's more a case I wanted to work with them because they are great artists, and all, without exception, have more than a little of an edge on the live side.

I'm still a sucker for the live performance.

The reason I recall those few examples is because I think they demonstrate, that as an agent, what you need to do is do what you do as best you can and hopefully it will serve you well. We've certainly been lucky enough to work with some of my favourite artists and there are still several artists who I'm a big fan of and would like to work with.

★

The other main category of artists is the new artists; artists you pick up on at the beginning of their career. For me, these were people like Nanci Griffiths, Robert Cray, The Roches, Stevie Ray Vaughan, Iris DeMent, The Buzzcocks, The Undertones, The Human League and Hothouse Flowers. These artists were all out there waiting for us, and, as an agent, we are turned on to them by friends, record companies, other artists, cassettes in our mail bags. All we need to do is to have the ears to listen to them, the eyes to see them and be prepared to follow our instincts and convictions. People are generally passionate about their music and equally passionate, in a negative way, about the music they don't like.

Passion is infectious.

As an agent, when you discover a new act you start on a mission to convince as many people as possible of the artist's brilliance. You'll ring up a promoter and rave about the artist. With luck he'll remember all the other artists you've (hopefully) been right about, and he'll be prepared to take a chance by joining you in the age-old promoter & agent partnership of finding an audience for the artist. If he's as convinced as you are, then he'll go off and vibe up all of his contacts, eventually getting that vibe through to the public.

A friend of mine in America sent me a copy of Nanci Griffiths' first album. This particular friend, a musician, was not involved in Nanci's career in any way. As they say in the business, "There was no percentage in it for him," but he thought I might like her music; he was 100% spot on, I loved it. I made contact with her manager and did a deal to bring her over. On her fist visit she sold 74 tickets out of 100 in the Mean Fiddler Acoustic Room. The album sold a couple of thousand copies. She returned to Ireland and England quite a few times over the following several years, until she regularly had gold albums in the UK and Ireland, and because of the strength of her live shows she could sell out a week at the Olympia Theatre in Dublin (7,000 tickets in total) and three nights in The Royal Albert Hall in London (15,000 tickets in total).

Nanci has gone on to enjoy a long and substantial career, but in terms of longevity she's the exception rather than the rule as far as female artists are concerned. I'd have to say, from what I've witnessed, it seems to be a lot harder for female artists – we're talking serious artists here by the way – to (a) get started on a career and (b) to keep it going. I call it the "Frill is Gone Theory" and it probably has something to do with the music business being a male dominated industry. It just seems to me that there are lots of great talents out there – I'm not going to insult them by listing names – who have made beautiful albums and given amazing concerts but seem to have just disappeared.

Female and male acts benefit immensely from breaking out of the live circuit. It seems to me that artists whose success comes as a direct result of playing live enjoy much longer careers than say artists discovered and thrust upon us by the record industry. We've already discussed how Nanci Griffiths started. Robert Cray was another artist whose career and record sales were driven and led by his success in concert venues up and down the country – as is the case with all of the above artists though, people like Hothouse Flowers and The Undertones also enjoyed several Top 10 singles as well.

Thankfully, the live scene is not a scene that fades. There are always great people out there and it's our job to find them. To me, that has always been one of the most exciting parts of my work; finding new artists.

It really is such an incredible feeling to find something new. I remember back in 1978, someone from Good Vibrations Records in Belfast sent me a copy of The Undertones' first EP *Teenage Kicks*. The first time I played it, the music knocked my socks off. I played the EP non-stop that weekend, loving every second of it and checking if it would stand the test of time, and not be like a McDonald's kick. But no, I needn't have worried, John O'Neil's songs were classics in the making. He has a way of saying something that is very simple and obvious, but something you wished you'd had the gumption to say yourself. On top of which, he has an ear for melody, which mainlines the song directly into your brain. The actual recording showed the band to be a raw powerhouse, driven by chunky chords on the guitar. On record, they created a very pleasing sound, not unlike the sound The Beatles made in the early days. The following Monday morning, I tracked them down and I picked up a bit of a Roches vibe from them – you know, they were suspicious of people in the business. A week or so after that, I was in Belfast for a Van Morrison concert and The Undertones came down from Derry to meet up with me at my hotel. They had that vital, for me, band vibe. They looked like they were meant to be together and their humour, mostly at my expense it has to be said, worked as team humour. They looked like if it ever got to be an "us" against "them" situation, then the "us" of The Undertones would win hands down every time.

The important question I always ask a new act is who they are fans of.

If they are passionate fans of other artists, then I always feel they have a chance. If, like The Boomtown Rats, they state – whether or not they believed it didn't matter – that "everything else is shite" then, I feel, you're on a sticky wicket immediately.

I discovered The Undertones loved Val Doonican, Bridie Gallagher and Ronnie Carroll . . . no, just kidding . . . they loved Them, The Buzzcocks and The Ramones. After that we had a hoot together and didn't really discuss business. A week later they confirmed, "Of course we'll go with Asgard, sure haven't you got The Buzzcocks." That's really how it happens a lot in this business. New people feel that if you're good enough to look after their heroes, you're good enough to look after them. And that was how we came to represent them right through their original run. They delivered some amazing concerts and some amazing records and then they made a tactical decision that they didn't want to end up on the chicken-and-chips-in-a-basket circuit, so they quit when they were on top.

Later they reformed, without Fergal Sharkey, which was definitely their decision and right, but personally I felt it was a big mistake.

It's always better to discover your own acts though. You should never try to short-cut your career as an agent by nicking another agent's artist, which brings us back, quite nicely, to our contract issue. Talking of which, as an agent, *always* sign your artist; *never* sign the manager. The manager may get fired, or he might make so much money he retires, so *always* make your contract out directly between you and the artists themselves.

"Yes, yes, yes," I hear you moan, "*but what does an agent actually do?*"

Okay, most people kinda know that agents are responsible for getting artists some kind of work. Anyone who's seen DA Pennyfather's classic study of Dylan, *Don't Look Back*, actually experienced an agent at work. I'm sorry to say that Mr. Tito Burns, with his Terry-Thomas influenced performance, didn't do much for my profession. I believe it was Tito who, on one momentous occasion, was overheard saying, "How do you expect me to make a living when my artists take 90% of my income?"

But apart from what it appeared Mr. Burns did in *Don't Look Back*, what most of us actually do is find our artists and then find work for them in the performing arena.

An agent will represent several artists – an important point to remember this one.

Okay, so what will the agent do for Goggles Anonymous, a band we've already shown who has some kind of a fan base? Around the time Goggles Anonymous is going to release their new album, they are going to have to tour, to bring the same said album to the attention of their loyal fans. The two opposing views at this stage will be, whether you should tour before the album, so that you build up an anticipation for the album and subsequent sales, or whether the album should be out for a few weeks before you start the tour so that (a) people will be aware of your newer material and (b) the profile of the new album will have helped you sell more tickets for your concerts. As an agent, I believe in the latter, but somehow the record companies always seem to win this particular argument by shifting the goalposts after tickets have gone on sale.

The agent will have a conversation with the artist, the manager and the record company and eventually all will agree the length of the tour, the venues, the cities and countries to be covered. The agent will return to his office, contact the promoters he knows in each city of the planned tour, and have them check out the availability of the various venues. The promoters will send the availabilities through to the agent and the agent will then build the tour around the availability, the routing, and the artist's preferred touring schedule. Most artists have a preference for three consecutive nights of concerts, one night off, three nights back on, one off, etc., etc. It's an exact science, based on strength of lungs, strength of character and desire to get it all over with as soon, or as late, as possible. James Taylor likes a break after every second concert; on the other hand, Mark Knopfler really hates dates off and rarely allows them to appear in his schedule. In this instance I suppose it's a case similar to the one Loudon Wainwright III once sang, "*If the day off doesn't get you, the bad reviewer will.*"

The longer the notice, the greater the availability of the venue, and the greater the availability of the venues, the easier it is to build a well-routed tour. Artists appreciate tours well scheduled in conjunction with a map, as opposed to those put together by throwing darts at the map in your office.

If your agent asks, "What's a map?" I think you might have a problem.

It's a bit like the time Coliseum (Jon Hiseman's jazz fusion band) turned up to play their gig in Newcastle-under-Lyme, only to (eventually) discover they were meant to be playing at Newcastle upon Tyne. It's as easy to get it wrong as it is to get it right if you don't pay attention to detail.

According to Ed Bicknell, Dire Straits encountered a few teething problems with their early agent. The group was booked by their agent into a Swansea working men's club. Let's not forget that they were critically acclaimed right from the start, so it wasn't even that they were playing their way through the working men's clubs. Anyway, in Swansea after the opening turn (support artist) but before the bingo, they set up their gear and did their full set. They enjoyed a pretty indifferent reaction from the distracted audience. They concluded their set to near silence, and were happy to seek out the sanctuary of the dressing room where they began changing out of their stage gear. They took it all in good spirits and even joked about it as the roadies started to break down the stage. About 20 minutes later, the club secretary comes into the dressing room.

"Isn't it about time you lot got back out there and did your encore?" he enquired, twiddling with his waxed moustache.

When the band realised the club secretary wasn't joking, they started to protest about how lukewarm a reception they had received and that the last thing that particular audience wanted was another number from their fabulous repertoire.

"Oh don't be deceived by that lot; they really liked you and besides, everyone does an encore here," the club secretary said, and then proceeded to state, for the record, all the turns who had played at his club and how each and every one of them performed their encore.

Despite the band's protests the secretary stood his ground and eventually demanded the band fulfil their contract and play an encore. So, about 40 minutes after they'd originally finished their set, and after the road crew had set the gear back up again, the band took to the stage in a tidal wave of indifference and performed their solitary encore.

The same luckless agent booked Dire Straits into a one-off in Dundee University for the princely fee of £70. The agent had obviously been unable to find a show either on the way up to or down from Scotland to help break the journey. The band had given their word to perform, so they drove the whole way up to Dundee, only to discover that the Social Secretary had mistakenly booked the band outside term time. Rather than have driven all that way just to turn and go back home, the band decided to play the gig anyway, so the crew set up their gear to play. They ended up playing to only eight people. They were lucky even to get that number. The manager had to fight with security to persuade them not to throw out three troublemakers.

But all bands have such stories, and such stories and mishaps help to shape the band and the crew. If you are on the rise, like Dire Straits were, then it's easy to take all of the above and more in your stride. Indeed such adventures can result in some serious bonding between musicians and crew. But if you've been on that same circuit for a couple of years and feel you're going nowhere, then all such cock-ups will serve only to sow the seeds of dissent. And the most annoying thing is that there will always be one musician or crew member who will appear to take great pleasure in being the bearer of doom and gloom. The fact that he or she is part of it won't come into the equation. It seems that such members take a perverse pleasure in rushing into the dressing room and deadpanning:

"Ah well, Dire Straits played here last month and only drew eight people. Now considering they have an album out, our audience of six is not too bad."

The other band members will be tempted to agree with Dennis Dissenter, and, just as they're starting to feel not too bad with thoughts of, "Goodness, we must be going places after all, if we can draw 75% of Dire Straits' audience," Dennis will add: "Mind you, I think they had eight *plus* the bar staff, whereas our six includes the bar staff!"

No one will dare ask how many bar staff are on duty. But an albatross like Dennis Dissenter should be fired at the earliest possible opportunity.

Agents don't go out of their way to find dates like these two examples. Sometimes, for some acts, sadly that's all that's available. Mostly though, when you're starting, they'll come up – with the help of the aforementioned map – with something a bit more presentable and for the example of our book let's assume he'll present Goggles Anonymous with something resembling a proper tour.

Perfect routed tour under his arm, the agent then goes back to each of the promoters and advises them of the ideal night for their particular city. The promoter pencils the venue for that night and submits a costing to the agent. The costing – I've included sample costings for Hammersmith Odeon, see page 107 – will basically show the capacity of the venue and the ticket price. We multiply the capacity by the ticket price and we have the gross for the concert. We divide this amount by 1.175, which give us the total box-office-take after VAT (Value Added Tax) has been deducted. The costing will also incorporate lists of the expenses incurred in staging the concerts. We then subtract the cost of running the show from the box office (after VAT) figure and we have the net amount left to be split between the artist and the promoter. Usually the artists will receive a guaranteed fee against a percentage of the net. The percentage can be as low as 75% of this net to the artist, and 25% to the promoter, or as high as 97.5% to the artist, and 2.5% to the promoter. It's even been rumoured that on The Rolling Stones 2003 tour, they were charging some promoters 102% of the net. Perhaps they were trying to find a way of cutting themselves into all the little side deals, such as bank interest on advance ticket sales, concessions, the bars, the car parking, the booking fee on the tickets and indirect sponsorship deals.

Once the agent and the promoter have spent a suitable amount of time haggling about how the net should be split and what the guaranteed fee should be, the gig will be officially termed as confirmed. The agent will then issue contracts. The contracts will cover all of the above details, plus a payment schedule – how much is paid in advance, how much is paid on the night – and the artist's contract rider. The agent will send a copy of this contract to the manager/artist and a second copy of the contract to the promoter. Both parties will sign and return the contract to their agent. The agent will then send the artist the promoter's signed copy of the contract, and the artist's signed copy of the contract will be sent to the promoter. Phew!

With the concert now fully confirmed, the promoter will then officially book the venue and pay a deposit to secure the booking. He or she will then put the tickets on sale and print leaflets and posters advertising the concert. For this they will use only artwork approved by the artists. The promoter will also place and pay for adverts in the local and national press, advertising the show. He and the agent will monitor the ticket sales, and place additional adverts or have the artist do additional interviews as ticket sales, or lack of them, dictate.

The agent will continue this process throughout the country, the rest of Europe or the world, depending on the stature of the artist. He will also keep his eye keenly on the artist's career, and ensure that, concert-wise at least, the artist is always seen to be taking a step in the right direction. Well-paid spots with good billing on festivals can see artists take several steps up the proverbial ladder. A bad performance at a festival or a duet with Michael Bolton will see them slip back down the snake.

As the agent continues with his master plan, the promoter will be attending to the business of promoting the concert and preparing for the big night. Every artist's contract that's sent out contains the artist's rider (see example on pages 189–193). The artist's rider is a list of requests peculiar to that particular artist. The promoter has to pay great attention to these details and, invariably, the bigger the artist, the more ludicrous the demands.

Apparently Madonna, when introduced to promoters at her concerts, always informs them that they will hear from her only if she's unhappy.

Artist's riders list how many stage crew will be required to help empty the artist's truck(s) and set up the gear, a process which will be reversed at the end of the night. The rider will also list the artist's catering requirements; exact billing; the number of guest tickets they'll require; parking requirements; security requirements; hotel accommodation and internal transportation requirements − *if* these have been included as part of the deal. Then, on the night, the promoter and his staff will stage and run the concert and deal with the artist mostly through the road crew and tour manager. At the end of the night, he or she will settle up with the artist's tour manager or road accountant, depending on the stature of the act and pay over the balance of the fee plus any percentage, if appropriate.

The agent doesn't need to attend each concert but the promoter really should. If he can't, then he will have a representative (known affectionately as "the promoter's rep") to deal with all of his responsibilities. The agent will turn up from time to time, in times of trouble or glory.

The agent will liaise with all of the people involved with the artist, and in instances where neither a manager nor a record company have been appointed, the agent will help make the connection and generally vibe up the necessary parties.

So, where do agents come from? In the Seventies and the Eighties the majority of London agencies filled their vacancies with ex-Student Union social secretaries. Some of the more ambitious social secretaries saw agencies as their short cut into the glamorous music business and many of them have now progressed into the higher echelons of the industry.

But that was then. That well-worn path is now completely exploited. Nowadays, I would say, the best way for an agent to start would be to go out and find your own act and work your whatsits off, building them to the extent that people in the industry begin paying attention to them and, consequently, you. Another route would be to start your own (little) agency and little agencies have a habit of growing into big ones when one or more of their artists break (i.e. becomes successful), at which point the little agency (agent) will be bought up by one of the larger agencies who are perhaps not quite as successful on the talent scouting front. But you soon discover finding your own acts is always the best, and most satisfying, way to be an agent.

And for those would-be-agents probably the most important bit of advice I could offer would be to *live on the telephone*.

Live on the telephone. Sure, emailing and faxing is fine and efficient and allows you to distance yourself and have a hands-off approach, but in the agency world, there really is (still) no substitute for the personal touch. You're not going to pick up much gossip via email or fax – no one wants to be seen to be committing that kind of stuff to paper, but when you get on the old blower the first thing will be that the promoter will be so shocked to be actually speaking to a real live agent on the phone that within minutes he'll be giving you the low-down on what's happening and what's not, who's happy and who's not.

Don't forget, the promoter and/or his rep gets to see what's going on behind the stage, away from all the PR and Razz McTazz. He's going to know who's going to want to be on the move, who's happy with their agent and why, and who's not happy with their agent and why.

If you're interested in keeping your artists, it's mostly down to Elvis and the Colonel's famous big "TCB" (taking care of business); you take care of your business and look after your acts properly and you stand a better chance of continuing to represent your artists.

Sometimes it's hard to take care of your artists to their complete satisfaction. Procol Harum were booked to play at the Blizen Festival in Belgium. They were due on stage at 22:00 hours they thought. Their agent, Doug Darcy from Chrysalis, arrived in a stretch limo at 21.45 to see his charges on and off the stage. By 03.00 hours though, they still hadn't appeared, so the band gaffer-taped Doug's mouth, legs and hands and deposited him in the bucket of a JCB – don't bother to ask what a JCB was doing so close to the stage. The band then had him hoisted up into the air, where he stayed until he was rescued at 10:00 hours the following morning, by which time the band had played their long overdue set and disappeared into the dawn in Doug's limo.

But back to the telephone – live on it even if you've got nothing to sell. Get into the habit of getting into the office early in the morning and not dreading the telephone work but looking forward to it. There are an awful lot of promoters out there and they all pretty much know what's happening in their area. The ones who are more tuned in use the better local artists for the opening spots. That way they get to hear about the new bands before the buzz starts. Promoters, in turn, know the good agents to recommend these new bands to; conversely they also know the ones to steer them clear of.

In the early days baby agents were called bookers but nowadays everyone seems to be an agent.

But no matter, if you're an agent or a booker, go to gigs, go to lots of gigs. This may sound like an obvious thing to say to an agent, but I think I got a lot of my early breaks because I'd been out on the circuit (with Fruupp) and I knew all the promoters face to face. Then when I rang them up, I wasn't just another of the London agents – well with my accent I was never going to be that – but they knew me, bad jokes and all. So, having that personal contact can only work to your advantage can't it?

I remember when I was trying to get started I didn't have many acts, two in fact, Fruupp and Gnidrolog. One was un-pronounceable and the other was (and probably still is) unspellable. So let's just say that the agency commissions weren't really thick on the ground so I had to look around for other ways to supplement my meagre income.

One of the ventures I actually considered was knocking on the doors of houses trying to sell paintings.

I went to this hippie kind of meeting which was made up of desperate people such as myself and this kind-of-guru, one of the owners of the company selling artwork. And this girl had it down to a T. All the dos and don'ts. She kept repeating these points over and over:

1. Don't be pushy.
2. Don't disagree with a potential customer when they criticise the painting.
3. Equally, if you like the picture, don't be scared to say so and why.
4. Never give the impression that you *need* to sell your painting.
5. Try and get into the house and sit down and talk to the customer.
6. Don't feel the need to talk about making the sale, talk about yourself and ask about the customer.
7. Never have a pitch, never use standard or regular patter.
8. Never feel bad if you don't make a sale.
9. Try and put yourself in a position to be able to call back with another painting.

I never went back a second time even though she had performed her personal spin on me, religiously following her nine key points, and had tried to convince me to go and work for them. It was commission-based work, which at that stage it wasn't particularly attractive. I might even have gone back – maybe not to try to sell paintings – were it not for the fact that when the meeting broke I spotted our guru being collected by another guru and they looked like they were off to star in a painting of their own.

I've only really thought about this again recently but, really, she could have been, in her high-powered yet seductive chat, preaching the gospel of how to be an agent.

I would of course have to add another point to the nine . . . well agents like 10, don't they? It's their magic number; it's easy to divide and multiply by.

Anyway my addition would be:

Always fill your date sheets.

It might seem a bit obvious to you, and to a degree, it is, but you'd be surprised by the number of tours that go out, on every level from the Half Moon Putney to Wembley, with play days missing in the itinerary. Nothing puts as big a smile on a manager's face as a full date sheet.

No matter their problems, and we certainly had a few, Fruupp always had a full date sheet, mainly because the fewer the gigs, the less the income, and guess who was the last one in line when it came to dishing out the wages? Yes, yours truly.

One of our early agents at Asgard used to handle a band called The Chords, and their manager used to come into the agent's office and stand for hours looking at the map going, "There must be somewhere else we can play." And usually there was.

So, if you're an agent and your act is up and running, always remember, no matter how much your act enjoys hanging out with you socially, they'll love you even more if you fill their date sheet.

In short, an agent's main job seems to me to be that of a *convincer*. He starts off by (hopefully) convincing an artist to work with him. He then has to convince a promoter to do what they don't want to do, which is to take a gamble on a new artist they've never even heard of. Finally, when the pendulum has swung entirely in the opposite direction, he has to convince the successful artist who'd be just as happy to stay at home, or in the studio, to come out and do concerts that they really don't necessarily want to do for the promoters.

Some days you bite the cigar; other days the dog bites you.

5

THE BIG PIE

Before we continue with who else can help you achieve success I suppose we should briefly examine where your (financial) success will come from.

RECORDS:

There are two main sources of income from your records.

(a)   The person(s) who perform on the records – the recording artist(s) – receive record royalties. This royalty generally works out at about 30 pence per single and about £1.20 per album.

(b)   The person(s) who wrote the song – the songwriter(s) – the above artist(s) recorded will receive songwriting royalties. This generally works out somewhere in the region of 51 pence per album.

A & B need not necessarily be one and the same. In the case of Bob Dylan, The Beatles, Ray Davies, Paul Simon and Van Morrison, where the performer is also the writer, obviously it is. But in the case, for example, of the majority of boy bands, girl bands, combos – boy and girl bands – Bob The Builder, Cliff Richard and Elvis Presley, they are not. I mention both Elvis and Cliff to show that you need not necessarily record your own work to be mega successful.

So, every time a record is sold, the performing artist will receive a small payment (minus deductions, which we'll go into later) and the songwriter will receive a small payment. On top of which, every time the record is played on the radio, television and stage, a small payment will find it's way back into the performer's pocket and the writer's pocket via the various collection societies, PRS, PPL, GVL, Amadi and Sami.

62

But let's get back to *your* records.

Every time one of your songs is used in a movie or for an advert, the record company *and* the publishing company will be paid a bunch of money – sometimes as much as £100,000 in each instance!

Depending on your deal, a certain amount of this will make its way back to the writer (via the music publisher) and to the performer (via the record company).

LIVE INCOME:

For concert appearances you will receive income and we'll go into the breakdown of that later, i.e. where the money comes from and where it finds its way to.

TELEVISION AND RADIO APPEARANCES:

Not a lot of income here I'm afraid. For instance, for an appearance on *Top Of The Pops*, a four-piece group will be paid, in total, about £500. It will cost as much in expenses for them to do the show. Once you hit the Celebrity 'A' list then a different set of television shows will become available to you, most of which will pay top dollar, particularly those on the European mainland.

Generally though, all TV and Radio appearances, if you're lucky enough to get them, are gold-dust, in that they are treated as promotional vehicles which will help you sell your records, and if you sell lots of records then you can work out from the above how much you'll receive.

MERCHANDISING: SWAG

Swag (Stuff We All Get) is the term used to describe the merchandising you will see on sale at any concert venue. Items like t-shirts, baseball caps, sweatshirts, posters, brochures, patches, transfers, badges, key-rings, pens and tour jackets will all be graced with the band's logo and will be on sale at quite high prices. The majority of successful touring artists make a very healthy income from their swag. Ticket holders at the concert will hand over anything from £2.50 to £16.00 per person for their souvenirs. If we're talking about a concert at Wembley Arena, with a capacity of 10,000 (plus) that's certainly enough to keep your manager in fine claret for a couple of months.

SPONSORSHIP DEALS:

Sponsorship deals are deals made with a rather large company, who will pay tons of money to you just so their product can be associated with your high media profile. This can be as little as £25,000 on the low end, and (literally) into the millions on the high end. We're talking here about sponsors like Pepsi and Volkswagen. The rule of thumb here is that these people usually only want to pay you this money when, in theory, you need it least. I know, I know, when do any of us *not* really need money? But let's just say, when you need money most, i.e. when you're starting off your career in the music business, sponsors will be as rare as a silent roadie.

Those are your main areas of income.

Now you know where your income is going to come from, we'd better start you on your way to earning it.

In selecting your team, though, no matter whether you're talking about agents, managers, publishers or record companies, what matters is that you should do all your groundwork and research in secrecy. Try not to make enemies by having a list of people waiting for your call, only to turn them down. It's better to come onto the scene as someone's fresh project, rather than have a crowd of people you rejected who will say bad things about you if only because you turned them down. You won't have the time or the energy to negotiate your way through a minefield of enemies later.

6

THE MANAGER

Okay, so we have our band, we have our songs, and we have our agent and we know where our income is going to come from, so, let's talk about our manager.

Your manager should be a very creative person – someone who can discover, invent and break an artist. It's vitally important that your manager share your vision and your passion.

All great acts have had great managers.

Good examples would be Larry Parnes and his extensive stable of stars; Colonel Tom Parker and Elvis Presley; Jake Riviera and the other Elvis; Peter Grant and Led Zeppelin; Ed Bicknell and Dire Straits; Paul McGuinness and U2; Miles Copeland and The Police; and, *of course*, Brian Epstein and The Beatles.

I know it's very popular these days to claim that Brian Epstein negotiated some bad deals on The Beatles' behalf. I'd have to disagree with that. He was ploughing new pastures; he was doing deals that had never been done before. Since then, of course, those pioneering deals have been bettered. We're talking 40 years ago so we'd hope so, wouldn't we? I mean it didn't really take long to develop the wheel once it had been invented. But the invention, now that was *the* thing! Without Brian Epstein, I believe much of the artist power evident in the current music business wouldn't exist. Before Brian Epstein, many managers were the stars. As far as the artists were concerned, what the manager said was gospel. Some managers took 50% of the income, some even paid the artist nothing but a weekly salary, and still the majority of those artists said, yes sir, no sir and three bags full sir. To a great degree, Epstein changed all of that . . . and changed it forever.

The question you have to ask yourself is, why did U2 work and bands like Simple Minds (whose nickname used to be U3) and Alarm didn't? On paper at least all three bands were cut from the same cloth with their urban anthem style music. Again, on paper at least, you'd have to say that, at the start, U2 had the weakest of the three record companies. And, yes, maybe with *The Joshua Tree*, U2 *did* move into a different gear, but how did they get to be in the position to find that particular rare gear when the other two didn't? The only answer I can come up with is management.

From the very beginning, U2's manager had a vision, and a plan, and manager and band had the confidence to keep to the plan. It's very easy to look at them now, when they are mega and everything is hunky-dory, but let's not forget they paid their dues, and big time. They all sat in the back of a van together on the breadline chugging around the various countries.

From the outside, as with a marriage, you can never really know the balance of power. You know, whether the manager has a vision and follows it, or, if the manager is at the beck and call of the band.

Johnny Rogan in his enlightening *Starmakers And Svengalis* book, lists what he feels, are the 13 different types of manager.

The Autocratic Manager
The Concerned Parent
The Indulgent Manager
The Neophyte Manager
Poachers and Inheritors
The Neutered Lackey
The Dilettante Manager
The Fatalistic Manager
The Over Reacher
The Scapegoat Manager
The Dual Role Manager
Co-Management and Team Management
The Record Company Manager

Because I'm slightly suspicious of that unlucky-for-some number 13, I'll add two more types of managers to his list.

The Simon Fuller, I'm going to make *me* a Star, Manager.
The JFK Manager.

The JFK style manager should, I feel, be high on your wish list of managers. Like Kennedy, you want someone who already enjoys a bit of power/clout. Someone who will act as a good Chairman Of The

Board and will, on your behalf, canvass all those who, supposedly, have the knowledge, collate all the information available, and then, when in possession of all the facts, decide on a plan or a direction. Added to which, don't forget that it's quite possible there are going to be situations where the artist will overrule the manager, and the manager will still be expected to act on the artist's behalf, even though it's against their better judgment. It takes a special kind of manager to carry this little manoeuvre off successfully .

Now, I suppose one of the decisions you have to make should be based on whether you felt JFK or Nixon made the better President of The United States of America. Do you want someone like JFK with his thoughtful, considerate but brain-picking-cum-nicking style, or do you want a Tricky Dicky with his much maligned, "Look, I know what's best for you. I know how to do this. The end justifies the means. The medicine is bitter, but the cure is perfect, so STFU while I get on with it."

STFU? Okay, the clue is it's usually seen above the stage in jazz clubs, the first word is "Shut", the second word is "The" the last word is "Up".

I haven't added Nixon to Mr. Rogan's original list as an additional type because I feel Tricky Dicky is lurking in there somewhere already.

I'd say the single most important factor in choosing a manager is appointing someone who really cares about you and your music. Experience of the music business isn't really a necessity because your manager can be kept on the right tracks by your solicitor, accountant and/or agent. Don't go looking for the star manager; don't go thinking, just because he did it for Madonna, he'll do it for you. The music business graveyard is littered with artists who were star managers' pet projects. If you think about it, you're on a hiding to nothing if you take that route. A Star Manager *can* walk into his pet record company with any new band and win them a deal simply because of the number of units his main act is shifting. However, that's totally the wrong reason to sign to him. He can't get an audience to like and/or buy your music. If we're talking about your group, then I'm sure you'll find that when the record company starts working on your project, they are not usually committed to you in the way they need to be for you to have a chance of success. You are seen, and tarnished, as an indulgence and traditionally they'll do just enough to keep the star manager off their backs.

So choose someone who totally believes in *you*. Don't feel you have to make a decision overnight. Hang out with your prospective manager and get to know him *extremely* well; throw him a few curved balls and see how he deals with the wobbles, and do your deal with him *only* when you are 100% convinced of his commitment to you and your music. Remember to choose carefully – you could be working with this person for the next 20 or so years of your life, which is substantially longer than most people stay married these days.

I believe it's better to have no manager at all than to have the wrong manager.

What do you need from your manager? As I have said before and I'd like to stress here again, you really need someone who shares your vision and belief in your music. They should be able to deal with lots of different kinds of people. On numerous occasions you're simply not going to have the time to meet every single person who is involved in your career. You're not going to have the time to sit in on every marketing meeting, and even if you did, you should still avoid them like the plague. There's just not the time to meet all of the German licensees, let alone the licensees of the 50 other territories you may be lucky enough to have your records released in, *but* you still need to be represented on these occasions. If your representative acts like an egotistic moron, I'm afraid you will be tarred with the same brush. The bottom line in this business is that there are too many people queuing up for these people's time and attention and money, so if you put one foot wrong, you'll find yourself at the back of the queue again. Just in case you're thinking, "Oh well, not to worry, I'll just wait until I get to the front of the queue again for my next chance," don't! Don't even dream of that – it never happens.

In a manager, you need someone who can rally the troops. You need someone who can be firm and decisive, someone who can cut through all the crap and hype and bullshit this business throws up daily. You need someone who can just as easily be Mr. Nice Guy, as someone capable of throwing the full Corgi-wobble when necessary. (The half-Corgi is the manager sitting up on hind legs, front paws paddling as if in the water, and doing lots of barking. The full Corgi is where any hint of politeness is immediately dispensed with, and the manager goes straight for the jugular. A fine example of the full Corgi can be found in Led Zeppelin's movie *The Song Remains The Same*, during which heavy-weight manager Peter Grant verbally attacks a concert promoter whom he suspects of permitting a pirate merchandiser to sell photographs of the group within the venue where Zeppelin are performing.) You need someone who can scrub up well for certain occasions. Someone who

68

can hold a conversation with complete strangers beyond discussing football and the weather and someone who realises that there are times to party and times not to party, but, most importantly, in case you missed it first time round, someone who has a vision for you, your music and your career.

Managers should be resourceful and adventurous. Yes I suppose, even a little like a swashbuckling pirate. The award to the manager in this section would have to go to one Mr. David Robinson, manager of seminal Brinsely Schwarz and, with Jake Riviera, co-founder of Stiff Records. Dave was certainly a bit of an entrepreneur and (like all pirates) he always had an eye out for a (bounty) bargain. He traced and bought a barge in Holland and went over to check it out before parting with his hard-earned cash. The barge was perfect for his requirements and he agreed the price. The seller offered to have the boat delivered to the UK for an additional £875. Mr. Robinson – who'd never sailed a boat in his life – said: "Nagh, I don't foresee a problem. I'll take it home myself."

So Captain Robinson pulled into the docks (in his newly acquired barge) at the Hook of Holland Port. He waited, bobbing up and down in the water, until he saw a ferry heading for England and he merrily followed it home.

★

But now ladies and gentlemen, *the* big question? **How much will you have to pay your manager?** The quick answer is 20%. Around a fifth of your earnings will go to your manager. Now there are numerous variations on this. Some managers will demand 25%, which doesn't mean you should agree to it. Other (apparently) more reasonable managers will have a commission rate of 15%, which again doesn't necessarily mean you should agree to pay it. It's rather low, and you want your manager to be exactly that, *your manager*, and someone who will donate all their time and energy to you. If he's receiving a mere 15% commission, financially speaking he may find it hard to resist taking on other artists as well, which, as we'll discuss later, may not necessarily be in your best interests.

To me, it's always seemed fair and reasonable that a manager would take 20% of the artist's gross receipts on records and publishing because it's clear profit for the artist. However, you might want to try and get them to take 15% or 20% of the *net* of your live earnings, i.e. after you've paid all your on-the-road-expenses. I suppose the fairest way to look at it is that you should expect your manager to take commission on what you take home, and not what you're turning over.

You have to realise that if you achieve any degree of success your manager is also going to be in the front line when it comes to temptation.

Ed Bicknell was sitting in his office one day minding his own business, i.e. keeping an eye on the Polyglots to ensure they were continuing to sell his turn's – Dire Straits – albums by the proverbial truck-load, when Jean, his PA, buzzed him on the intercom to announce that there was a strange looking Spanish promoter in reception wanting to have an unscheduled meeting with him. Keen for a bit of entertainment, Ed asked for the promoter to be sent up to his office. The Spaniard walked into Ed's office, carrying what looked like a snazzy James Bond style briefcase. He announced he was staging a three-day festival in Marbella. He claimed he'd already booked Queen and The Moody Blues and he wanted Dire Straits to headline the Saturday concert.

"Have you ever run a show before?" Ed asked.

"No!"

"Where is the show going to be?"

"In a football stadium."

"Have you got a proper stage with a roof?"

"It never rains in Spain."

These are the often-repeated words and, it should be recorded, the words feared most by managers and agents. They are usually delivered in either thick Italian or Spanish accents.

"Have you booked security?" Ed continued.

"No yet!" (You'll just have to imagine the Spanish dialect)

"Have you organised toilets and water and amenities for the audience?" Ed continued. He used to be an agent himself, so he knew all the right questions; equally he knew the answers he wanted to hear. Actually he started out his career as a drummer with The Average White Band – he was fired from them just because he wasn't Scottish – but that's another dialect.

"No yet," the Spanish promoter replied, growing more and more nervous by the second. For some strange reason he kept looking over his shoulder.

The promoter also seemed to be growing increasingly frustrated by Ed's incessant questioning.

"Who's backing the festival?" Ed asked.

"I can't tell you that," the promoter replied, in a voice barely above a whisper.

The promoter started to look around the room suspiciously again.

"There's no one else here," Ed said, refusing to be distracted, "who's backing your festival?"

"I can't tell you."

"Sorry," Ed laughed, "if I'm to send any act down to Spain to play at a festival, I need to know exactly *who* is backing the festival."

"Okay, I'll tell you," the promoter whispered, leaning over towards Ed's desk and so close the Dire Straits' manager could smell his after-shave, "The Arabs!"

The promoter sat back up in his seat with a gesture, which suggested, "I never said that". He kept looking around the office, up at the ceiling and at all the pictures on the wall.

"It's okay, it's okay, the room's not bugged," Ed said, laughing out loud at the developing farce.

The promoter seemed to take comfort from Ed's assurance. Then he stood up, unfastened his briefcase, swivelled it around on the desk so the open end was facing Ed and slid it so it stopped right under the manager's nose, all the time his right eye twitching furiously.

The briefcase was packed to the rim with wads of cash!

"What's this?" Ed asked.

"It's for you!"

"What is it?"

"It's money!" the promoter replied, surprised that his (numerous) pennies hadn't dropped.

"I can see that, how much is here?"

"One hundred thousand pounds!"

"Is it for the band?" Ed asked, thinking that the promoter had brought part of the fee in cash – foolish to the nth degree of course as they'd never met before or ever discussed a deal.

"I don't think you understand," the promoter smiled, his right eye accomplishing successfully what it had been trying to achieve for the past few minutes, winking, not twitching, "it's for you!"

Then Ed realised what was going on. The Spanish promoter was trying to bribe him. He couldn't believe it. Before that point, when he'd been an agent, he'd occasionally been offered the odd fiver, which he'd laughed off and sent the offender away with a flea in his ear. But for someone he'd never met to walk into his office with £100,000 in cash and just want to give it to him beggared belief.

He shut the case, money still within, handed it back to the promoter, took the telephone number of the hotel the promoter was staying in and promised he would check out the festival and contact him again if he felt it was suitable for his act to play.

The minute the promoter left Ed's office, he was on the phone to his mate, Jim Beach, who managed Queen.

"Here, are you guys doing this festival in Marbella?" Ed asked Jim.

"No way," Jim Beach laughed down the line. "Does this mean that the dodgy promoter with the briefcase has just been around to see you too?"

Ed received the same response from The Moody Blues' office and all three managers enjoyed a quiet chuckle when, three months later, a certain high profile artist topped the bill at the aforementioned festival!

*

By now things are clicking into gear for Goggles Anonymous. Say for the sake of our discussion, the single caused a bit of a stir. It has been given airtime on a few radio station play lists around the country. Maybe you'll even pick up a few television shows. That, plus your gigging, has created an audience for your debut album, which enters the charts in the Top 20. You should be quite happy, but not ecstatic, with your progress to date; you're on target, but only just. Things are about to become more complicated. And with the increase in your profile, you really should now start to seek out and appoint a manager. With your new profile, you'll now have no problem finding a different class of manager interested in you.

The likelihood is that there will be so much going on that you won't be able to keep on top of it. This is obviously the most vital point in your career to have a manager. Later, when you have broken through as an artist, a caretaker manager or PA (personal assistant) will suffice, but right about the time of your first album charting, you will have a platform and an opportunity from which to successfully launch your career. As well as building and consolidating your UK career, you've got to consider other European territories. Experienced managers know how this system works; they know how to exploit it to your best advantage. Basically, the system necessitates climbing up on the bucking bronco and hanging on for dear life. If you are still mounted when the bronco slows down, you'll have done well.

After Europe, America, the most romantic of territories, will beckon. Historically, it has to be stated that no matter how big a group/artist become in UK/Mainland Europe, if they don't break America, they seldom last. Of course there are exceptions to every rule, but I can't think of many. You might suggest Cliff Richard and then I'd say that 'Devil Woman' reached number six in the American charts. He also had two other American Top 10 hits, so perhaps Cliff had America in his grasp and just chose to let it go, I really don't know. On top of this, few artists have had a European career to surpass Cliff's. Would Slade, T. Rex, Boyzone, Jam and all of the Brit Pop bands have split up, if they'd conquered America? I think not. But the main point here is that if you've left your choice of management until now, it's preferable to appoint a manager who has American experience. If that's not possible, all is not lost, simply appoint one who agrees to work with a co-manager in America.

In America, management is all about TCB – taking care of business. I suppose this could be interpreted one of two ways. Supposedly one US manager kept the plastic covers on the sofa cushions in his apartment because it was easier to wash the blood off that way!

I prefer to believe that TCB is all about follow-up; it's about living on the phone. It's about being on the case, *taking care of business*. With the time difference between Europe and America (NYC is five hours behind the UK, and LA a further three hours behind NYC) it is nigh on impossible to do it successfully from the UK. Few have managed to accomplish this remarkable feat; where many have failed. Successful American Management leaves nothing to chance. They won't be happy with you allocating them only four weeks of touring once a year. The only way to break America is to go over there regularly and work it, work the concert circuit and work the radio stations. There are no short cuts. The reason Elvis Costello was the most successful of all the so-called UK punk acts, was because Jake Riviera, his manager, understood the American way, and their entire operation would regularly decamp to America for six months at a time. But unfortunately there are few Jake's around. Miles Copeland (Police & Sting), Ed Bicknell (Dire Straits) and Paul McGuinness (U2) spring to mind, but the problem is they are not necessarily right for you or your act. You need to find a new Jake, Ed, Miles, or a new Mr. McGuinness. I think these are the four greatest managers of my generation. All have entirely different approaches and styles, but all are totally motivated and artist driven. All have steered their charges to global success.

Jake Riviera was, and is, a totally fearless manager. He is completely and utterly committed to his artists and their work, and heaven help you if you get in their way. With Jake, there is no hidden agenda. It is a battefield out there. It's a battlefield he enjoys. It's "Chocs away and over the top" and he's right there in the trenches, fighting with his artists.

Around 1985, following six UK top albums and 13 Top 30 singles, Elvis Costello was in a position where his recording contract had run out. They'd already decided not to renew with the existing companies, so Jake Riveria started negotiations with several labels. One of the labels that made a lot of noise about signing Elvis was Virgin Records. Richard Branson was personally making the running, lots of telephone calls, letters and faxes, about how he'd love to have Elvis, about how Elvis is the most important artist blah blah blah. So Jake goes for a meeting with Richard on his barge. Richard starts straight in to a rap about what a big fan he is of Elvis, blah blah blah and so Jake says, "Okay Richard, tell you what, name me the titles of three Elvis songs that weren't singles, and I'll sign a contract right here and now with Virgin."

The outcome of that meeting was that RCA Records added *another* Elvis to their list.

In my career, I have managed The Blues By Five, Fruupp, Radio Stars, Van Morrison (Business Arrangements was the exact title Van afforded me; Pee Wee Ellis did the Horn Arrangements for Van and I did the Business Arrangements), Gerry Rafferty, Dexy's Midnight Runners and Tanita Tikaram. With all of them, except Tanita, I was a caretaker manager. I started out as their agent, that's what I am, that's what I do, that's what I enjoy doing and that's what I'm proud to be. On the remaining above acts, there was no manager around at the time, so I was pulled in to take care of management duties.

Mostly I enjoyed the work. I have to admit here though that I resigned from Dexy's after about a week. It was around the time of their *Don't Stand Me Down* album and pretty soon I realised that the only reason they wanted a manager was to have someone around who'd be prepared to say, "No!" to the record company on their behalf.

All of the above artists were people whose music I loved and, just like the early days, someone was needed to help them put their show on the road. I try to avoid such a situation these days. I describe the role only to show you that at the juncture in Goggles Anonymous' career that we are now discussing (their first album threatening to take off big time) a caretaker manager is exactly what they don't need. They should hold out until they find the right person and, as I say, with help from your lawyer, your accountant and your agent, you *will* find someone. Again I've included a few names at the back, but I would remind you that when you are interviewing anyone, it is of vital importance that you are their number one act. No matter how much you may appear to like the manager's presentation and pitch, if they are managing several other acts at the same time, then do yourself a favour and strike them off your shortlist immediately.

Managers are always on the lookout for new clients and at any time in London there is sure to be a meeting going on between strangers in pursuit of clients or managers.

Chris Morrison and Chris O'Donnell managed Thin Lizzy, amongst others. On one memorable occasion they were going for a meeting with Ray Davies and had arranged to meet up with him outside a gym.

"How will we recognise him?" Chris "Murray" Morrison asked C.O.D.

"Ray Davies! How will we recognise Ray Davies? Sure isn't he only the biggest and best pop icon alive today," C.O.D replied in shock.

"'I wouldn't know him if he came up and bit my hand off," Murray replied nonchalantly.

About 15 minutes of general chitchat between the two mates later, this bagman wanders towards them. He was a real down-and-out, but for some reason he had a bit of a sparkle in his eyes.

Quick as a flash C.O.D. offered his hand to the bagman and without batting an eyelid said, "Ray, good to see you again. My goodness you look like you're in a bad way. Boy do you need a bit of good management."

The blood drained from Murray's face and he turned to walk away as C.O.D. continued the farce by holding a conversation with the bagman.

Eventually, joke over, C.O.D. let the bagman continue on his journey, his right hand warmed and a couple of pound coins the richer.

A few minutes later, the very dapper Ray Davies himself arrived and the three of them headed off for their meeting.

7

THE TEAM

"Our record is recorded," Philip Dansette, the lead singer and song-writer of Goggles Anonymous shouts. "We're about to release it. Do we need a publisher for my music?"

Good question Philip, and good time to talk about the Music Publishers and the rest of the team you will need to put together to look after your interests.

Why do you need a Music Publisher in the first place?

Well, nowadays you need a publisher to protect the copyright of your songs and to collect the income they generate around the world. This income will mostly come from your record sales, but it can also come from other people doing versions of your songs, your songs being used in movies, on television and for adverts. This is what music publishers do for you these days. They're pretty much like a bank in that they will advance you money against the above listed income, which they will collect. The only problem is, like banks, the music publishers will charge you for this privilege – they'll deduct anything from 10% to 40% of your income. At the top end, this could be considered unfair, unless of course they are also going to do for you what music publishers used to do.

In the good old days, that is to say, in the days of Tin Pan Alley, you had people who wrote songs and you had people who recorded songs and rarely were they one and the same. So the music publisher's job was to secure "covers" of their client's songs by other recording artists. Then along came Chuck Berry, Buddy Holly, Lennon & McCartney and Dylan, and the shift to artists recording their own songs started. By the Seventies it had become the norm and the power had shifted away from the music publisher.

There are still a few of the old-fashioned music publishers around, people like Peter Barnes, Stuart Hornall and Kenny MacPherson, who are not content with the income generated by the artists recording their own work. So they go out to secure additional covers by other artists. Tom Waits often says his songs are like his children – they grow up, go out into the world and make a living for him. If you can find a Peter Barnes, a Stuart Hornall or a Kenny MacPherson first and foremost interested in pushing you and your career as a songwriter – great. That's definitely the way to go. If not, don't sign just yet. Release the first record under Copyright Control, which means that the song(s) is registered directly to you and all the publishing income will go directly to you. If that single is any size of a hit, that's the time to do your publishing deal – when you're hot. You will receive a much better deal from the publisher – a higher advance and a bigger royalty.

"What can I expect from a publishing deal?" Philip Dansette asks.

If your first song is a hit, then anything from £100,000 to £250,000 is not unreasonable. Percentage-wise, most publishers will want to deduct 15% to 20% for the privilege of collecting your songwriting royalties on your behalf. They will, of course, pay you a large chunk of it in advance. Some publishers will even drop their share to 10%, if you push hard enough and you are hot enough. By the way, just in case you think I was completely serious when I mentioned "the good old days" of publishers earlier, it's worth noting here that in the good old days the publishers took at least 50% of the songwriters income.

Back to dealing with today's publishers though. The important thing to write into the contract is that all the song rights are returned to you after say five years. This way you keep all of your songs under your control.

And just to set the cat amongst the pigeons, ask them – the publishers that is, not the pigeons – if you can have a share of the Black Box Fund. Such a fund actually exists and it's where all unclaimed royalties and percentages from different collection societies end up. Publishers share out the black fund amongst themselves; no artist that I am aware of actually participates in this revenue.

You're starting to think about deals so you should also start to think about taking legal advice. You need to pick a **lawyer**, that's a solicitor to you and me, but the music business side of the legal profession likes to be known as lawyers, like their American counterparts. Your agent can recommend a few names, so can your manager. The golden rule is never to choose a solicitor who also acts for your manager, your agent or anyone else you are involved with. I'd meet a few lawyers first if I were you before making a decision. I've included a few names in an appendix at the end of the book. These are all people who specialise in the music business. But, at the end of the day, it's really down to you and how you get on with them. Meet them, chat with them and see if you like them. It doesn't matter how great their reputation is if you don't like him, or her, don't ask him to work with you. In putting your team together I think it is vital to have at least one person involved who is a constant. Managers may come and go, agents may come and (won't want to) go, but lawyers and accountants, once in place, should stay. Apart from anything else, they get paid by the hour, so all the advice they give you will never be based on how much commission they're going to make on a deal. Throughout your entire career, you'll find it very comforting to be able to go back consistently to the same person to run things by them. So, what I'm saying is, try to choose your lawyer, or accountant, with some of the wisdom and expertise you will expect to receive from both of them.

Next comes the big one: *your record company*. The company of people who will help you get your music out into world and into your fans' homes, relieving them of a little of their hard-earned cash in the process.

You've done a few shows and the A&R guy from the record company has started to pay attention. A&R stands for either "Artiste & Repertoire" or "Arrange & Record" (there seems to be two schools of thought as to the origins of the title). Anyway, the A&R guy is the artist's first contact with the record company. He is the guy, or gal, who spends all his or her life either in a darkened basement listening to demos, or in small dingy clubs listening to groups. They rarely see the sun! The A&R Manager is the talent scout, whose job it is to find talent for the record company to feed into their hungry and very expensive machine. Today it's Goggles Anonymous' turn to draw the attention of the scouting department and pretty soon the A&R officer and someone from their business affairs department will start to negotiate a deal with you or your representative(s). No matter who your representative(s) may be, always take part in these negotiations yourself. Sometimes the buzz of a record company simply being interested in you and being pre-pared to release your work is enough to ensure you sign on any dotted line which is put in front of you. BUT we're talking here about your music, and quite possibly a big chunk of your life, being tied up with the company in question, so force yourself to take an interest and an active part in the negotiations. If your lawyer and the business affair's person start talking in legal gobbledegook, don't be scared to say, "Hang on a minute, but could you run that by me again, only this time could I have it in English please."

If you're a new group and you've created a bit of a buzz, **your recording contract deal memo** could read something like:

1. Commitment: One album firm, with four further one-year options for an additional album each year. (Which means that the record company are committing to you for one album, whereas you are committing to them for five.)
2. Advance (recoupable against royalties):
   £100,000 for first album
   £125,000 for second album
   £150,000 for third album
   £200,000 for fourth album
   £300,000 for fifth album.

Sadly, most artists don't even bother to read beyond these figures.
They're out of there and off on a shopping spree, leaving manager and lawyer to tie up the deal. But, for those who do read on, the deal memo will continue:

3. Recording costs to be agreed in advance by the record company and deducted from future royalties.
4. Video costs: Video costs to be agreed in advance by the record company and deducted from future royalties.
5. Territory: The World.
6. Tour Support. Tour support – the shortfall between the fees you receive and the money you have to pay in expenses in order to undertake said tours – to be agreed in advance by the record company and deducted from future royalties.
7. Duration of contract: Until a year after the fifth album has been delivered.
8. Royalty Rate: (This doesn't really mean very much. Record Companies don't mind giving a high percentage and then taking some of it back from you within the contract. They legally use packing deductions, returns, promotional copies, free copies, record clubs, foreign sales and reserves to reduce your royalty rate. So always ask your lawyer or your record company, "How much exactly do I get in my pocket for every album sold?" If the figure is in the £1.20 neighbourhood you're on the right track. But please

don't forget that very important question, "But how much money will I be paid for *every* record I sell?" Tell them you're not in the slightest bit interested in reading paragraph upon paragraph detailing the deductions they will make from your royalties, that you don't care a fig about wholesale and retail and packing deductions, and gross and net and overseas currencies, and the price of fish in Katmandu. In all of this you have to remember that you're new to this. Don't allow them to make you feel intimidated. The record companies have had a 50-year head start on you. That's not to say that all of them are out to take advantage. The great ones will completely understand and try to accommodate you as best they can.)

All you need do in your negotiations is ensure that the deal is one you will be able to live with. If you are afraid that your record royalty rate is too low, then say so at the meeting. Suggest they introduce an escalation clause once you achieve a plateau of sales. For instance, if your first album sells 250,000, the record company will have received a fair return on their investment, so in your initial negotiations, suggest that they increase your royalty rate by ½% when you sell 250,000, and then an additional ½% when you reach 500,000, and maybe an extra 1% at 1,000,000, and an extra 2% at 2,000,000 and an even further 2% at 3,000,000. All of which would give you an extra (and realistic) 6% when (and if) you were to achieve three million sales.

As I mentioned earlier we managed Tanita Tikaram. I saw her do her first ever show at the Mean Fiddler in December 1987. By the end of July the following year, she had her first Top 10 hit with 'Good Tradition'. I mention it here only because when we were doing the initial negotiations I requested a royalty escalation such as the one I've outlined above. When I reached the 3,000,000 figure, Mr. Warner and several of his Brothers were rolling about on the carpet in hysterics. Through their tears of laughter, they said, "Paul, if Tanita ever achieves 3,000,000 sales, of course we'll pay her that royalty." Within two years of signing the contract, sales of Ms. Tikaram's very fine debut album, *Ancient Heart*, coasted past the 3,500,000 sales figure, and Tanita achieved her superstar royalty. Mind you, she earned each and every penny of it. I know just how hard she worked for her success.

For me, the major imbalance in the deals offered by most record companies is the issue of who owns the masters. Record companies should pay for the masters if they want to own them. But they never do, do they? Yes, they pay for the master in advance, but then they deduct it from your money (royalties). Artists should own their own masters. It's their birthright, their bloodline, whatever you want to call it, and if that's not reason enough for you, then the artist should own the master simply because they've paid for them. Yes, the record companies can say that they have to pay for the recording of the masters up front, and in fact that's perfectly true. So what you should say is, "Okay, fine, you (the record company) can own the masters and pay us a royalty until such time as you've recouped your costs, at which point, and for life thereafter, the ownership of the masters reverts to us, the artists, and we will then lease the masters back to you." This is certainly not a situation that will be changed overnight, but if enough artists hold out in the negotiations with the record companies on this point and for as long as they possibly can, then eventually the record companies are going to have to give in on it. And that's the point when the power will swing back to the artists, where it belongs. It's really as simple as that.

It seems to me that the other main bone of contention in a record deal is the issue of under-reporting and under-accounting. Under-accounting is where the record company will, in the royalty statement they give to you twice a year, literally report only a percentage of your albums sales. This seems to be causing more of a stir currently in the USA. Under-accounting is where they don't pay you the full money due to you on the sales they are reporting. I mean, as if the contract you have with them isn't already biased heavily in their favour, they have to go and do this as well. Of course once your accountant conducts an audit on their figures, they will re-assess the situation and pay you on your *actual* sales. You'd think that made it fair, wouldn't you? Fair that is, until you realise that a full audit can cost in the region of £10,000, a figure not every artist can afford.

Patrick Savage from OJ Kilkenny & Company, one of the UK's best music business accountancy firms, told me that in his 15 years in this business, 95% of the audits of record company's figures he has carried out on his artists' behalf have revealed that the record company in question *has been* under-reporting the artists' record sales. That is to say that the record companies have not been paying the artists their full and true due. As I say, when these mistakes are pointed out, the record companies will pay the difference. But they will not pay interest on the difference, nor will they reimburse you for your audit fees, unless you can show that they are under-accounting to you by a figure of 10% or more. In order to keep some kind of fairness in this, Pat Savage also advised me that in the same 15 years he has only *once* discovered a situation where a record company over-accounted to an artist and this was for only a few thousand dollars. (On another separate occasion he discovered a situation where a major record company over-accounted to a smaller record company who it was acting as distributor for.)

So this would kind of lead me to believe that the record companies see under-reporting and under-accounting as a standard industry practice.

Of course it's most unfair to the artists who can't afford the fee to carry out the audit. You know, where the £10,000 audit turns up only £5,000 for the artist. Obviously that is not a risk an average artist can afford to take. At the same time, the missing £5,000 is not a sum the same artist can afford to write off.

The thought that worries me the most in this, though, is whether all this means that there are certain delegated record company staff who sit around and figure out which artists they are going to under-report and by how much.

There's a word for that, isn't there? And isn't it illegal in most civilised countries?

If there is staff sitting around discussing under-reporting, are they the same members of the record company staff who the artists also have to sit down with and discuss various other aspects of their careers?

The record company is meant to be your partner, so why would they do this to you? Easy, they do this to you *because they can* and more importantly, *because it's not an illegal practice*. Make under-reporting and under-accounting an illegal practice with penalties and the record companies will stop doing it immediately.

Perhaps I'm just overly suspicious and in Pat Savage's 15 years of audits he was discovering genuine mistakes.

But just in case that wasn't the situation make sure when negotiating your recording contract that your representatives include access for auditing and also try to include a clause whereby the record company *has* to pay you 10% interest on the amount (if any) they are found to be under-paying you.

Now don't go feeling too sorry for the record company, with this bit of hammering we've been giving them. I've never seen a poor record executive; I have however seen lots of poor musicians. When you are doing your deal, remember, the top executives in UK record companies are currently receiving anything between £100,000 and £1,000,000 per year *plus* bonus. When your career is long gone, they'll still be earning that kind of money. I find the distribution of funds grossly unfair. I think it's about time a bigger percentage of the income began finding its way back into the musicians' own pockets or purses, where it belongs.

This is not an issue about money; it's about *protecting* the money and your right to the money you're generating in what is historically a short shelf life.

These are probably issues you'll get around to addressing later on in your career, when you've sold a few million albums, but it's very important you are made aware of them. If artists could only be encouraged to keep bringing up these issues in the initial negotiations then, bit by bit, things may change for the better. For now though, let's get back and see how Goggles Anonymous are getting on.

The better A&R managers will, like your agent, also have a good network of contacts, so they'll be able to put you in touch with managers, agents, lawyers, accountants, etc., etc. The A&R department will also help you make your record, help you choose producers, engineers, studios, musicians and help you select your songs.

In all of this, the thing you should be most careful about, the thing you've got to be the most precious about is *your music* and the people who work with you in the creative process of putting that music together for a record. Really, you get one chance to get it right, and then it's down on your album for prosperity and you'll never be able to change it. Success has many fathers, and if your music is successful, you'll have a whole army of people ready to jump into the spotlight to take the bow for your success. Conversely, failure is quite simply a much-maligned orphan.

When Warner Brothers first signed Ry Cooder, they signed him with the knowledge that they would have to release a few albums until he broke even and started to cover his costs. As it turned out, it took about seven albums before the classic *Bop Til You Drop* turned Ry's account from red to black. These days, you get one chance, two if you're very lucky. In fact, the same company released only one Little Village album. I wonder if this had anything to do with the fact that the debut album didn't achieve the accountants' expectations? Little Village were Ry Cooder's Nineties' supergroup, featuring Mr. Cooder, Nick Lowe, Jim Keltner and John Hiatt. Sadly they made only one album; figure that one out if you can?

Another thing we have to accept and realise is that record companies don't always get it right. Take for instance the famous Underground period during the late Sixties and early Seventies. Warner Brothers went out actively looking for *their* very own Beatles. Capitol Records had The Beatles, Warner Brothers didn't, so they decided they would go out and sign their own group to emulate The Beatles. Now, in a lot of instances, Undergound music was a euphemism for artists who hadn't quite got it together in either the songwriting or playing live areas and, perhaps, putting this as politely as possible, should never have been signed to a record company at that particular stage in their career. Warner Brothers were fearless though, and they wanted and needed their new Beatles, so that's why artists like The Fugs, The Electric Prunes, Harpers Bizarre, Arthur Writus & The Nagging Pains, Mephistopheles, Wilderness Road and The Beau Brummels found themselves with record deals. Mind you, it should also be stated here for the record, that it was also around the same time that the very same Warner Brothers signed Van Morrison, and released *Astral Weeks*, which I believe is one of the best contemporary music albums ever to have been made.

But I think in this case, the exception proves the rule, and apart from Mr. Morrison, we had some questionable music enjoying a certain degree of success.

But how can such poor music have been successful?

Easy. You take a case like the one above with Warner Brothers, where the record company actively go out and try to *create* something. If they are that desperate they are as likely to sign a crap act as they are a class act. It's a general rule that record companies who don't have ears for good music, don't seem to care how much they need to spend signing crap music. Consequently, this means that their initial exposure (signing on fee and recording costs) is so great, they just have to go out and prove themselves correct by spending loads more dosh promoting their new acts.

"Okay," I hear you say, "that's fine. I can see the logic in that, but why do people then go out and buy this music?"

If you promote anything heavily enough, someone will buy it; that's really the simple but sad answer.

The marketing department will be instructed to go out with all guns blazing, to ensure the record company recoups their initial investment. The press department of a record company will have their "company-friendly" journalists, who will always cover what needs to be covered to ensure continued access to CDs and free trips to exotic locations around the world to review and interview the big artists.

Now it may not be as devious as all that; there are journalists out there who want to be the first to discover someone new, someone their fellow journalists don't know about. Apart from which, just go into any newsagent and look at the thousands upon thousands of pages that need to be filled daily, weekly and monthly. The journalists have to write about something, and they're like everyone else, they want to try and grab attention, and if that means knocking someone big, or praising someone obscure, then so be it. Jon Landau famously wrote, "I've seen the future of rock'n'roll and it's Bruce Springsteen." It hasn't exactly proved to be an accurate prediction but Jon subsequently became Bruce's manager, so perhaps every *crowd* does have a silver lining.

Anyway, a music fan picks up a credible paper and reads something positive about someone like . . . well anyone really. Pick your least favourite act, right? And then the music fan in question goes off to check out the new music. There are a group of people out there who love to be the first on the block to know and buy new music. There's a bit of this type of person in all of us, isn't there? On top of that there are some people who actually seem to enjoy crap music.

The main problem the crap acts create is to clog up the system for your favourite act or, in this instance, for Goggles Anonymous. So Goggles Anonymous need to be extremely careful with the people they decide to work with.

In the recording process, producers are obviously one of the most important elements and often the hardest to find. Take your time to research on your producer. Meet up with them as many times as possible; try to get to know them as best you can. You need to be able to assess if they'll be prepared to help you achieve your artistic goals, or if they are going to want to go their own tried and tested route because they think it works. That's part of the magic of having a wee bit of studio experience under your belt by this stage; you'll be familiar with the language, you won't be in awe the minute you walk into a room to start your record just because of all the other great albums that have been made there. Also be careful of the fan route. Sadly, too many artists want to make a record with Nick Lowe just because he produced the best Elvis Costello records. Try to find your own Nick Lowe or George Martin or Tony Visconti or whomever.

Once the album is completed, that's the last you'll hear from the A&R manager, until either the presentation ceremony of your first gold disc, or the ugly subject of remixing rears its head. The remixing scenario generally only happens when your first releases are not as successful as everyone had anticipated. The A&R person will return with a desire to fix it for you. Personally, I've always been of the opinion that if it's not in the grooves, no amount of remixing is going to fix it. But, you've got to seem willing, and anyway, you don't want to be appearing so negative to the record company's suggestions so close to the start of your career.

Album one from Goggles Anonymous is in the can, and for the purpose of this tale, let's assume the album has been well received. Before the A&R manager whizzes off to A&R someone else, he will introduce you to the rest of the team, namely the press department, the radio and TV promotion department and the marketing department.

And they'll all jump on to your career with unbridled enthusiasm. Please always remember that records do not sell by accident, so in the early stages, you should accept everything you are offered with a smile on your face.

Most of the major record companies now look like they are either specialising in cruise ship entertainment (Pop Idols) or they are closing up shop altogether. The British Record Industry is in an absolute mess and the only surprising thing for me is that people are surprised. As far as I can see, the record companies took their eyes off the ball in the mid-Eighties, when they, with their eyes fixed on their own bonuses, discovered a new way of making money. They didn't need talent scouts out scouring the length and breadth of the United Kingdom looking for new artists. They didn't need to spend money developing, recording, making videos, marketing and promoting these new artists. No, they realised all they needed to do was to re-release all the classic music of the Sixties and Seventies on the recently developed Compact Disc format. Not only did they not need to invest money to fund any of the above lists of expenses, they even had the cheek to go to the artists and say that they *wouldn't* be able to pay the said artists their fully negotiated royalty rate on the newly developing CD area. And you know what? In the majority of cases they got away with it.

And what happened in the decade they were milking the market? Well of course they stopped developing new talent. Yet, as we all know, new artists are the lifeblood of our industry.

Younger siblings reach a stage where they don't want to subscribe to the music their elder brothers or sisters are supporting. Of course not, they want their own *new* thing, and if it's not there what do they do? Yep. You've got it, they look for other pastimes to entertain themselves.

New pastimes like electronic games; sports – well, more importantly, sports-wear; personal computers and their games and communication opportunities; *anything* really. So music dropped from being perhaps the most important thing in the lives of Fifties, Sixties, Seventies and Eighties teenagers, to being "just another pastime" of the New Millennium generation.

I realise I'm probably oversimplifying things, but the facts and figures do certainly seem to support my theory.

The next mistake the record companies made was trying to buy their way out of the problem. When will they realise that neither they, nor television, can create artists? As we've already discussed, music is not something you can manufacture. Yes, you can dramatise developing artists competing against each other for television. But don't they realise that the only people who are going to enter these competitions are people who are desperate for success, who are craving fame, and motivated by money. They don't care how they achieve it. To such attention seekers, music is not a motivation or a calling. It is not something they *need* to do. Music is not something their lives depend on.

They are simply desperate to be in *show* business.

It's a bit like the two mothers in their respective gardens hanging out clothes at the clothesline talking about one of their sons.

> Mrs. Kelly: Aye, our wee Gerald is now in the entertainment industry.
> Mrs. Watson: Really, that's just great and what is he doing?
> Mrs. Kelly: Well, he's gone off to work with Smart's Circus?
> Mrs. Watson: Sure, isn't that just wonderful. You must be very proud of him. What exactly is he doing in the circus?
> Mrs. Kelly: Actually, he's working with the elephants.
> Mrs. Watson: Elephants! Incredible and what's he doing with the elephants, training them?
> Mrs. Kelly: Well actually he goes around after them with a bucket and spade picking up their . . . er . . . droppings.
> Mrs. Watson: Goodness Mavis that's terrible. Do you want me to see if I can get our Jim to get him a job on his building site?
> Mrs. Kelly: What? And have him stop working in show business? No way.

★

But getting back briefly to our pop rivals, reality television shows remind me, in more ways than one, of the Bob Dylan lyric: *". . . they're selling postcards of the hanging"*.

And, like the postcard of the hanging, you won't need or want more than one copy of the gruesome, but highly watchable event, so no one should be surprised when HearSay and their ilk die away after their first release. There's no real fan base, there's no investment from either artist or fans, so there's nothing left to hang around for.

The record companies have run aground because they've forgotten the artists *create* music and the record companies don't. That's the main difference and it's that difference that makes artists *so* special.

*

I also work with Eric Bibb and he's another artist cut from the same cloth as the exquisite roll that produced Rory Gallagher. He's blessed with the sweetest voice this side of Sam Cooke. On top of which, he plays acoustic guitar like he was born with it in his hands and he's never put it down since. As an agent, as with Rory, all you have to do is get him up on a stage and he does the rest. You book him into a venue and I guarantee that the next morning my phone will ring and it'll be the promoter raving about how great the show was and wondering when Mr. Bibb can return. It's totally a word of mouth thing, and over the last six years, Eric has gone from appearing in front of 60 to 100 people, to selling out the likes of the Barbican in London and similar theatres around the UK. He's repeating the same success in Australia and America where music fans have just started to be wooed by his charm. Now, about three years ago, he was with a major record company and even they could see this man's talent. But when Eric was about to tour his manager went to the record company for some support, you know, with simple requests like making sure they'd have the records in the shops and maybe even taking a few adverts and producing a few posters and leaflets to help sell the records and the tickets. The record company, point blank, refused the requests.

They didn't have it in their budget, they said.

But surely if you sell records you'll have a budget to work with, we said.

But we already sell records, they said.

But you can sell more records, we said.

But we might not, they said, and if we don't, we'd be cutting into our profits.

That's what you're up against.

But it doesn't stop there. All the time Eric was building a bigger and bigger live audience, and by this time this new audience loved him so much that they were desperate for his albums and they'd like to buy some, please sir.

Which you'd think is good, right?

Wrong.

The record company wasn't getting the albums into the shops, so the fans couldn't buy them.

Oh!

That's not fair, we say.

Okay, they reply, we'll tell you what we'll do. We'll sell the records to Eric and Eric can sell them himself at his concerts.

So Eric Bibb's canny manager, Alan Robinson, agreed and after just one tour he was shocked to see how many records, CDs actually, they were selling at concerts. He went off and did his sums and realised just how much money a record company actually makes per CD. And he thinks, "Well, if *we* were making that much per record, *we* could afford to produce posters and leaflets and I could afford to take adverts in the newspapers."

So that's exactly what he did. He and Eric set up their own record label Manhaton Records (Eric has a snazzy wardrobe of hats) and they've never looked back.

And it's not only artists like Eric Bibb who have gone this route. Chris Rea just released the record he claimed he was never allowed to make with his record label, and in fact I think in the end they refused to release it, so he put it out himself and, guess what, it sold by the proverbial truck load, and now he can't believe how easy it is and how much money generated from CD sales never actually made its way into his pocket. Simply Red, who over the course of their career have sold a good few records, have now also decided that the best way forward is for them to set up their own label. I wonder is it any kind of coincidence that Eric Bibb, Chris Rea and Simply Red were all on the same record label?

Artist owned labels are the fast growing cottage industry of the music business. When you are starting off your career the main problem is that you're not going to have the energy or finances to start your own label so you're going to need to find a record label to finance the recording side of your career.

There's a great article by Cree Clover, which I've listed in the

Bibliography. I'm not sure how easy it's going to be to get hold of a copy but if you're thinking of doing a record deal you should certainly try. It makes for very interesting reading and explains in great detail how recording contracts work and how the contracts don't always work in your favour.

Hey, don't get me wrong, it's not all doom and gloom out there. It's just that you have to be careful, and it's always handy to remember exactly who pays for the record company's lavish surroundings and lifestyle – YOU!! If possible try and cut the deal whereby you lease your music to a label. At least that way, if you have to move on you can take your catalogue with you.

★

But enough of record companies, time to recap here before we continue with **The Dream Team:**

Managers: We've dealt with them, so strike them off your list.

Agents: Ditto.

Lawyers and/or Solicitors: Are there to protect you legally and to ensure, along with your accountant, that all your business is in order. They charge by the hour, anything from £100 per hour for assistants to £250 – £400 an hour for partners. But in each project they do for you, get an estimate in advance. Never wait for an invoice to arrive to see what your legal bills are. They will deal with the legal issues in your contracts with Record Companies, Managers, Agents, Music Publishers, Merchandisers and Sponsors. However, you must still stay heavily involved yourself in all these and other issues of your contracts particularly the artistic matters.

Accountants: See also details in "Lawyers" above. Your accountant will also be responsible for giving you advise on tax matters, VAT matters, on auditing your various royalty statements and, occasionally, helping you protect your money in the long term. Again, I would not recommend that you permit your accountant or lawyers to set up a series of complicated companies to handle your income. Keep it simple; keep it very simple, that way it's very easy for you to keep on top of it. In all the deals you do with the people who pay you money (record companies; concert promoters; publishing companies; merchandising companies, etc.) have the contracts worded so that all funds go directly to *you*, and to *no one* else. In turn, you can then pay the invoices of those who provide you with a service. *Always* sign your own cheques. That is so important; important enough for me to mention again:

(a) Always have all your income paid directly to you.
(b) Always pay your own bills.
(c) Always sign your own cheques.

An accountant will charge you in the region of £50 (ish) an hour.

The Tour Manager: This essential individual is worth his or her weight in gold. Basically, a really good tour manager will help you and your manager co-ordinate the live side of your career. Some develop into either artist's PA, a manager's PA, a manager's partner, or a co-manager. A few even end up as managers themselves. But in the initial stages, they will take on only the responsibilities of the road work. You can find a tour manager either by promoting someone already in your road crew, or by hiring a freelancer. There are lots around. Your agent will know and work with the best and the worst of them, and will, hopefully, tip you off accordingly. They charge anything from £500–£3,000 per week while you're touring. If you require one to work for you exclusively, you will also have to pay him/her a retainer during the time you are not on the road.

The Publicist: Will be responsible for your press coverage or lack of it. Van Morrison once hired a publicist to keep him *out* of the press – or so the publicist claimed. They are either employees of the record company who work on you around the time your records are released, or you hire your own to look after you annually. The same goes for finding your PR firm as goes for finding your agent. Don't go with someone just because their firm also represents David Bowie or Paul McCartney; go with someone you feel knows what you are trying to do with *your* music and someone who you feel understands *you*. Make sure you are comfortable chatting to them. Independent PR companies will charge whatever they can get, but figure around £1,200–£10,000 per month.

The Record Plugger: This is the person responsible for getting you and your music on radio and television. It is vitally important to remember that, according to your plugger, if your song gets on the radio, it's because your plugger did a great job; and if your song doesn't get on the radio, it's because you've written a crap song. I've actually sat in a meeting at East West Records where the radio pluggers said, about a new Tanita Tikaram single, that the radio stations didn't want to play a particular song because it was too slow. "It's a ballad," he said, "they want TT to do something different." Tanita's *next* single was in fact an upbeat song. The same plugger reported, "They (Radio Onederful) won't play this," he said. "This is not what they expect from TT. They want a great big slow ballad from TT." I kid you not, that's what he said. Basically, you can't let it worry you. Radio stations play what they want to play and your plugger is only the messenger – to the Radio Stations with the music and to you with the bad news. As with The Publicist, some are record company employees, or if you wish to hire your own, they charge pretty much the same as the PR firms.

The Record Company: We've discussed them already quite a bit but maybe a quote from Robin Blanchflower (an A&R guy for a large record company) sums it all up as well as I could. He was sending a rejection letter to the manager of the group Japan, "This group has a lot of potential," he wrote. "Unfortunately we are not in the potential business." Worth noting here I suppose is that this was the same Robin Blanchflower who signed Fruupp to the label he was working with at that time, Pye Records. We were happy to go there just because they had been the home of The Kinks. Wrong reason!

The Publishing Company: We've also discussed them and I include a few names in the appendix.

The Merchandising Company: Sign with the merchandising company who will pay you most money in advance and who won't ask for some or all of it back again when you don't sell the volume they expect you to. At the same time, allow them only to produce items you would be happy to use yourself. Make sure you write lots of freebies into your contract.

Record Producers: Again, a very, very personal choice and it's probably wise to vary them from record to record. I know you're not meant to change a winning team, but then you also have to consider the boredom factor. For producers, I've included the names of a few agents who specialise in looking after record producers just to give you as wide as possible a selection but don't forget your A&R chap will want to have input in this area as well. Record producers can charge anywhere from £500 to £50,000 per track plus a royalty, with around the £3,000 mark being about the norm for someone with a bit of a reputation. Also worth checking out *The Art Of Music Production* by Richard James Burgess.

Road Crews: Definitely the guys who not only keep the show on the road, the wheels on the wagons but who also put the rattles back into the prams. Again, it's invaluable to you if at least a couple of them can work with you the whole way through your career. It means you'll always have a solid foundation to your crew. Most of the road crews I've worked with are loyal to a fault to their artists. One of the tour manager's roles is to help you put the road crew together. How much do road crews get paid? Never enough. So always pay them what you can afford to pay them. We'll also discuss road crews in greater detail later.

In selecting your team, *trust* is a word that is often used and it is a great quality to find in someone. For their sake as well as your own, never put anyone in the position where you are wondering whether or not you can actually trust them. So, set your business up so the word trust doesn't come into it. I've mentioned this before but it's certainly important enough to bring to your attention again. Word all of your contracts so that all the income owed to you is paid directly to you or your wholly owned company. In turn *you* pay the people who provide you with a service.

That's it, that's your dream team in place. That was easy, wasn't it?

Maybe yes; maybe no. To a certain degree, it's down to a wee bit of luck and a lot to do with great songs. In all of this, it doesn't really matter how good your dream team is, if you haven't got the songs. If it comes from the songs, you've got a chance. If you sit at home thinking, "The Music Business – that's a glamorous business, lots of girls/boys, lots of drugs, lots of booze and lots of dosh, yes I'll have a bit of that."

Then if I were you, I'd think again.

8

THE ART OF DOING THE DEAL

Assuming you've managed to find your way this far, you're now a professional gigging act. That is to say you are making a living from touring.

Ideally, you should be settling down into the routine of mixing your social life with your on-the-road life. It's not the easiest thing in the world to do but very important nonetheless. There are too many people who have become slaves to this touring lark and if they're not careful they wake up one day and discover that their life and a chance of genuine happiness has passed them by, never to come calling again.

The other thing that they could discover, if they're not careful, if they've not been paying attention to their business or their business associates, is that much of the income they've generated is no more, and just as no more as Monty Python's legendary dead parrot. Just like any other business that generates, potentially, large sums of money there are a host of people who will be eager to relieve you of some, if not all, of it.

So let's discuss this situation and let's – while we're about it – talk about the art of doing a deal. When you find out, could you please write and tell me. The secret here is that there is no secret. With regards to setting your fee, it's pretty much an exact science these days. As I'll show in the costings in the following chapter, you have your venue, you know the capacity, you know the ticket price, you know the expenses, so it's easy to work out how much is left to be divided up between the artist and the promoters.

However, there are a few tricks which promoters have developed over the years in order to skim a wee bit extra off the gross for themselves or to inflate the expenses so that the net appears smaller and consequently offers up a lesser fee for the artist.

There's a venue in Scotland which used to be very popular. It's a very nice house that a lot of people loved to play, and it had a generous capacity so you could take a good fee out of it. Then it was discovered that the venue had been pretending there were a couple of hundred less seats than there actually were. For a good few years they were skimming a considerable percentage off the top. The reason they got away with it? Probably something to do with the fact that the capacity they were declaring was, even with the deduction, quite a large one, so invariably artists were taking out more money than they were in many other venues outside of London. So the artists were leaving the venue with a large enough smile on their face, none the wiser to its true gross capacity.

Another popular method of depriving artists of their money is the Advertising Agency scam. Most promoters these days use an advertising agency to book their adverts. By virtue of the large volume of adverts advertising agencies place they benefit from discount prices offered by newspapers and magazines. These discounts rarely get as far as the artist. On one occasion, it was discovered that a certain promoter was a partner in the agency that was booking his adverts. Not only that, but his advertising agency was also charging a commission to the show.

THE TOP 10 SCAMS PROMOTERS HAVE BEEN KNOWN TO USE TO CHEAT ARTISTS.

1. Misleading the artist on the number of seats in the venue.
2. The Advertising Scam as outlined above.
3. In an unseated venue, printing up two sets of tickets, one set numbered 0001 to 1,500, and the second set listed 0001 to 1,000 and only declaring the manifest for the first set of tickets to the artist.
4. Claiming tickets are unsold, but not supplying the "deadwood" – unsold ticket stubs – to prove it.
5. Manufacturing their own receipts.
6. Inventing taxes.
7. Selling already used (torn) standing tickets by a side door other than the main entrance.
8. Claiming concert sponsors such as local media, radio or television companies have had complimentary tickets, when in fact they haven't; said complimentary tickets are subsequently sold, sometimes even through the touts at grossly inflated prices, *and* the promoter pockets all the cash.

9. Having suppliers inflate their invoices and splitting the difference with them.
10. Promoters who sell their allocation of comps (complimentary tickets) to a coach company for cash, claiming they have a lot of relatives from Blackpool.
11. Promoters who book a single billboard and present a photograph of the same billboard to the tour manager in each different city claiming major (multi-billboard) coverage.
12. A favourite in the Irish ballrooms this one – having been asked to supply a grand piano the artist turns up to find a battered old upright piano. "Of course it's a grand piano," says the promoter. "Sure didn't Jim Reeves use it."

(Indeed, Jim Reeves Irish Ballrooms piano stories are legendary in the Emerald Isle; and what do you mean, that's 12, what type of hands did you learn to count on?)

But as I said at the beginning of this chapter, at this stage, setting your concert fee is pretty much an exact science and your agent, tour manager and/or on-the-road accountant, will know where all the skeletons are buried. (If you're a promoter you know you're in trouble if the tour manager, while searching through your figures and receipts, declares: "Ah, what's this skeleton, the winner of the 1965 Sheffield Hide and Seek competition?")

The skill comes in settling on a fee for an event which is not governed by capacity and ticket sales. I'm referring to scenarios like multi-act festivals or Government or Council sponsored free shows. As in playing poker, the secret is to try and give away as little as possible of your hand (i.e. the minimum fee you are prepared to work for) while at the same time trying to steal a glance at his hand (i.e. the maximum the event is prepared to pay you).

As an agent the strongest hand you can be dealt is to have an artist who is not fussed whether they do the show or not. The minute the artist or their manager advises you that Goggles Anonymous *must* do a particular show, right there in that one word, you lose about 33% of your negotiating strength. It's quite similar to selling a house. If you *have* to sell your house you really have to take what's out there. If, on the other hand, you can afford to wait around until the *right* buyer comes along then you will always achieve your asking price.

But assuming your hands are not being tied, your opening gambit is to ascertain what exactly the promoter has in the budget for your act. This puts you in the driving seat to some degree. Unless he's an idiot, he won't immediately offer you the maximum. It's good though to let the promoter be the first one to mention a figure, at least you get the chance of laughing at the offer; if you handle it properly you'll be the one in the driving seat. You barter around as much as you think you can. Then you stall by going off to, "check if the artists can make the show", or whatever else comes into your head. This gives you a chance to do a bit of research into what kind of money is *really* out there.

Festivals are established artists' prime paydays, and, because the majority of artists enjoy a limited time in this arena, I feel agents owe it to their acts to secure the highest fee available for them. There's a good chance they'll never get to play that particular festival again, so it's not as if you'll have a chance at another time to redress the balance of a bad payday.

Never undersell your artist. Artists' fees go around the grapevine faster than viewers forget last year's Pop Idols. One booking on a badly paid festival can ruin your artist's earning potential for several years.

If, on the other hand, we're discussing a baby act, then a well-positioned spot on a festival can work wonders for their profile. You're not going to get a lot of money for it, so there's no use haggling over it. Grab it; confirm it on the spot, knowing the profile could influence your fees around the rest of the concert circuit. You'll hopefully get your chance at the big paydays later in your career.

Another tricky situation is the gig that your artist *really* wants to do — say a multi-artist bill or some other event. You'll be concerned about the deal. You know, the situation I'm referring to is when the promoters are assuring you that all the other artists involved are on a similar deal. It might be some kind of charity event so you don't want to be seen to be bickering and penny-pinching. Your safe way out of such a predicament is to invoke the Favourite Nations Clause, which means in effect that the event and/or promoter have to offer you the best deal they offer to any other artist taking part in the event. As, in essence, you're going to piggy-back someone else's deal, this little trick can also save your artist a fortune in legal fees.

When going about your business, never do a deal with anyone who tends to enjoy too liquid a lunch, particularly *after* lunchtime. You're going to have a hard time closing the deal, especially if he has his entire office listening at the other end of the phone and observing his performance.

With a business that is supposedly shady, I have to admit that I have been invited to take a walk down that particular overgrown path only twice in my career. Once it occurred when an American agent came right out and said it, "Okay the act's yours if you give me a piece off the top." We declined.

The other was with the manager of a big UK act, who was changing offices. He invited me to several lunches and teas and we talked and talked about us representing his act and joked and joked about the music business and what have you, but we never ever seemed to get any-where. Third parties hinted that they'd heard we'd taken on the act, but nothing was ever confirmed to us and eventually the tour was put together (without us being involved). Supposedly, at one of the gigs, a certain person was seen passing a brown paper bag to another certain person, the inference being that if during the course of the many lunches I had offered a brown paper bag arrangement, we would have done the tour. Truth is we'll never know because it's not something to which I've even given a second thought.

★

"You'll never work in show business again Sonny."

I've only ever had those immortal words spoken to me on one occa-sion. The speaker was Roger Forester.

What happened was that I had negotiated a deal to promote Meatloaf in Ireland. A promoter I used to work with in Ireland contacted me suggesting *he* should do the shows in the South of Ireland and *I* could do the shows in the North of Ireland. This would have been in Meat's (as his agent referred to him) first flush when he was mega everywhere, including Ireland. I declined this promoter's request, as you do, and then I received the call from Mr. Forester who was a friend of the same Irish promoter. At that time, Mr. Forester was the manager of Eric Clapton and really should have known better. But anyway, he got on the phone and politely, at first, tried to persuade me to pass the artist on to his friend. I refused, politely at first and then firmly, and that was when he uttered his, "You'll never work in show business again Sonny!" line. Obviously Mr. Forester's crystal ball wasn't working too well all those years ago.

★

Slight detour over, let's get back to the art of doing the deal.

I believe that Brian Epstein's *modus operandi* in the early Beatles days was, *It's more important to get the deal done than it is to do a great deal.*

How many times have you heard managers say, "Yeah, we could have gone with so and so" (please fill in the name of any of the major record companies here) "but they wouldn't give me a break on the packaging deductions." Or something similar. And now the manager and his act are still propping up the bar in the Mean Fiddler without a deal. Epstein knew that if he could expose people to the magic of The Beatles and their incredible songs, the music would do the rest, and if it took an average deal to get started, that was fine because he knew they'd soon be in a position of strength where they could renegotiate. Certainly, in that instance, history has shown us that he knew what he was doing. The Beatles became as big as it was possible to become, and none of them were short of a few bob.

When doing a deal, and we are now talking primarily about a record company deal, it's vitally important to know as much as possible about the personality of the person you are doing your deal with. As well as hearing what they *say* they have available to pay your act, you obviously need to try and find out what they can *actually* pay your act. It also helps if you know where they are coming from. For instance, you could have someone who works for the company, but as they are not *the* company, they could be so desperate to do a deal that will secure their bonus in the short term that they will pay you whatever you request for your act. Such characters are happy to cut a deal with you that, in the long term, might not be to their company's best advantage. For instance, he knows he's not going to be there in 10 years' time, so he doesn't give a shit whether you are, or not. He's keener to cop the glory of signing you and enjoying the bonus your short-term sales will provide.

A vital part of this chapter on the art of doing the deal is the art of compromise.

I have to admit in my case, I'm sorry to say, I seem only able to compromise when I really like the artists. Take for instance The Bill Graham, The Rolling Stones and the Slane Castle affair. When I first started to work with Van Morrison, the legendary Bill Graham was his manager. It certainly was a pleasure to meet the man who had near enough started the contemporary American coast-to-coast touring set-up. He was a larger than life gent; a big fan of music, a great storyteller, and his offices were an absolute must see for memorabilia fans such as myself. We got on well with him. Van's European tours were phenomenally successful, so the manager was happy. So happy, in fact, he even gave us a European tour with his other main client, Santana.

The Rolling Stones decided that having just completed a very successful American Tour with BGO (the San Francisco based Bill Graham Organisation) they were going to use the same promoters for their European tour. This decision seriously miffed Harvey Goldsmith (their normal promoter). At this point, we'd promoted two of the first multi-act outdoor shows in Ireland – The Police, Squeeze, John Otway, U2, The Q-Tips (actual billing order) – in Leixlip Castle and Dire Straits, The Undertones, Paul Brady and The Chieftains at Punchestown Race Track. Both sites were on the outskirts of Dublin, so we called them Dublin Festival Number 1 and Dublin Festival Number 2.

To be honest, promoting is not my first love. I love being an agent. It's much more exciting picking up on new artists and being involved directly, or even indirectly, in all aspects of their careers as they take off. On top of which the good weather factor ensures promoting outdoors is much more of a lottery. During the above two outdoor shows I found myself constantly worrying, not about whether or not enough people would turn up to pay the bills, but whether all the people who turned up would be safe enough. I mean, you put 40,000 on a field and *any-thing* can go wrong. So, in short, although financially speaking we washed our faces, as they say, I didn't find promoting the festivals to be an altogether pleasant experience.

Anyway, my mate at the BGO, Mick Brigden, threw into one of our many late night transatlantic conversations, mostly about Van, the fact that the Stones were interested in visiting Ireland and asked if I would come up with a few suggestions about where they might play. I lined up a few sites and the next time Mick was in London, we nipped over to Dublin to see a few prime locations, including Leixlip Castle, Dally-mount Stadium (whose general manager I remember as being a certain George Harrison, a different one though, although he was also a very warm chap) and ending up at Slane Castle where Lord Mountcharles was extremely hospitable and treated us to the best potato soup I've ever tasted in my life.

Slane Castle jumped to the top of the short list.

We're talking about the autumn before the scheduled date. Things were progressing fast. We received a 250 page manual on how to promote The Rolling Stones which was obviously very useful for a baseball stadium in the wilds of the US of A but totally useless for a picturesque field, bordered by a river and a Castle, in the wilds of Ireland. The Stones had two dates available to play Ireland; either a Saturday or a Sunday. I recommended a Saturday. Slane is a small village and The Rolling Stones or not, the locals would still want to go to Mass and/or church on a Sunday morning. The *BGO* people wanted to go with the Sunday.

They wanted to use an across-the-tour ticket price. I suggested a lower ticket price, which, I felt, accommodated the Irish market better.

They wanted to supply the tour support act, someone from America; I think it might have been the J Geils Band. Now I have nothing against the J Geils Band, but I wanted to see an Irish artist on the bill. I know it was probably me being a bit over-patriotic, but I like to see Irish artists on the major Irish events. It's kinda good manners, I feel, to invite the cream of the local talent when you're a guest in someone else's country. Apart from which Irish people love The Hothouse Flowers, Sharon Shannon, Luka Bloom, etc. and these artists will always give any international artist a run for their money up there in front of the home crowd.

As you can see we had three main stumbling blocks and Mr. Graham's lieutenants were on the phone every night saying we were going to have to back down. "Bill can't be seen to give way on these points," they said.

Basically, I felt they were being disrespectful to Ireland so I also refused to budge. Now, maybe what I should have done was to compromise and negotiate on the points. For instance, I should have been saying something like, "I can see why you'd like to use your tour support and I'm sure you can see why I'd love to use an Irish act, so why not put both acts on."

I could have followed that with, "I hear you about the tour ticket price, but let's actually examine it in detail. Let's look at the net. You know, when you go to Germany, France, Italy or England you're going to lose a percentage of your ticket price to local taxes and VAT. So, if you charge what I want to charge for tickets, you'll still come out of Ireland with more per ticket than you would in any of the other European countries."

That should have been my approach, then I could have finally hit them with, "And as I've given way on the first two points, could you please help me respect the local community and do your show on the Saturday and not the Sunday?"

But I didn't, and the reason I didn't, I figured out afterwards, was purely and simply because I've never been a fan of The Rolling Stones. I didn't care about them; I had no connection with their music and I didn't really care about trying to make their show happen.

Anyway, the show went ahead with Gentleman Jim Aiken promoting, and, as ever, he did a splendid job and they all lived happily ever after.

Did I have any regrets? No, not really. Well maybe just a little one when the next European Tour BGO presented was with Bob Dylan. Now I'm a major fan of Bob Dylan, always have been, always will be. For as long as I can remember, I have gone to see him perform every time he visits London. And you know what, if I had played ball with them on The Stones . . .

9

THE MONEY

If you've followed my earlier advice and already started to build up a bit of a following of your own, it's around this time that you will be offered the support tour option we mentioned earlier.

This is the unhealthy practice where a support act (in this case you) buys their way on to a tour. The record company foots the bill, again as an advance against future royalties, and all misguidedly believe it's a short cut to success. Firstly, audiences avoid support acts like the plague, preferring to remain instead in the theatre bar or a pub around the corner. Secondly, journalists seem to time their arrival at the venue at the exact moment the main act takes the stage. The buy-on can cost as much as £25,000 for a 20 day tour of the UK. On top of which, there are hotels, transportation, crew, rehearsals and the crew wedge factor to be paid for.

The wedge factor is where you pay the headlining group's sound engineer (the person responsible for the sound the audience hears in the venue), the monitor engineer (the person responsible for the sound the musicians hear on stage) and the LD or lighting designer (who is responsible for changing the lighting patterns on stage). This amounts to approximately a further £30 (and rising) per man per night.

I suppose it can be argued that what the support group does gain is experience in stagecraft. My own advice would be to get your stagecraft together somewhere less expensive. The only experience you will gain from this is how to play to half empty halls, which could of course, quite possibly, be valuable experience for later in your career when you've passed your peak as it were. In America, it's a completely different matter. Audiences are used to two-act and sometimes even three-act bills, so the support artists do get the attention (and the fees) they deserve.

The basic rule of thumb is never to pay to play. If your first gig is in a club and you receive a fee of £50, then make sure your expenses come to £37.50, leaving you with exactly enough change to buy another copy of this book to give to one of your mates. If you manage to get your fee up to £100, or £1,000 or even £10,000, the same thing applies – make sure you have change.

"Oh come on," I hear you say as you drool into your beer. "If I was getting £10,000 for a single concert, of course there would be change. I would be turning a fair old profit."

But you see, here's the thing, when you reach that level, you will find that there are other sets of pressures to deliver bigger and better shows. You'll have a road crew with a spending power of its own. You'll have a sound engineer who'll want you to go for the Rolls Royce sound system, you'll have a lighting designer who'll want you to go for the biggest lighting rig ever taken on the road; your tour manager will want a couple of assistants; separate sleeper coaches for the band, the band's crew, and the sound and lights crew; two, three, four or 10 articulated trucks will now be required to haul your gear around the country. No, that's not a truck that "speaks proper", that's a fecking expensive, and rather large, lorry to you and me.

Again, as with the initial record company meeting, make sure you're involved in all of the pre-production meetings where decisions are made regarding all matters related to your tour. Have your people spell out to you how much it's all going to cost. And, if you're lucky enough to be on a £10,000 fee, draw the line under all expenditure once it reaches £9,000. And then just sit back and watch the other £1,000 disappear on contingencies.

For the hell of it, let's just do a typical costing for a group who will receive £10,000 per concert.

Income (Per Show): £10,000

Expenses (Per Show):
Management commission:	£ 2,000
Agent's commission:	1,000
Accountant's fee:	200
Hotels:	750
PA Hire:	850
Lighting Hire:	650

The Money

Crew's Wages:	600
Band's Wages:	1,000
PDs:	300
Truck Hire:	500
Bus Hire:	500
Misc:	900
Total Expenses:	£ 9,250
Balance:	£750

You can usually do five concerts/gigs per week, so the above costs are based on that, which means that for the purposes of this costing, I've divided the weekly expenses by five to get the per gig expense figure.

PDs (Per Diems) are the £25/£30 food allowances the band and crew each receive per day. On top of which, on concert days, there will be free catering for you in the venue where your catering rider, which caters for your every whim including only green M&Ms – no that doesn't mean he's had a bad night, it's the little sweets we're talking about here – will be catered for.

All the rest is self-explanatory – I hope.

"But only £750 left for the artist out of the 10 grand, agh come on!" you scream.

"Sorry, but that's your bottom line," your agent will say as he adorns his asbestos suit.

"I know," you say, "you've inflated the Miscellaneous Figure to build in a wee bit for the artist, haven't you?"

"Sorry," the agent will say, "out of that miscellaneous figure, which is in the neighbourhood of 10% of your expenses, you've got to take into consideration: insurance; rehearsals; equipment hire and new stage clothes, if you're so inclined."

Just as the agent feels he's about to lose the tour, he'll add, "Obviously if you're on tour you'll sell truck loads of records, so you'll be up on record royalties and publishing royalties. Then there's the swag (merchandise). You've always been good for about 10 grand a week on the swag, haven't you? And of course if the tickets sell well, there's always extra money to be earned as you'll break percentage every night."

In all seriousness, please always watch your bottom line and never ever pay to play, no matter what level you're on.

Again, just so you can see how the £10,000 fee fits into the scheme of things, here's a semi-accurate breakdown of the kind of fees you can expect at the various venues:

1. The wee pub at the end of the road: whatever you take on the door, which might be £10 or might maybe even reach £100 if you have a great night.
2. The Pub Gigs on the circuit: either a straight percentage of the door which could get you as much as £200 or a straight fee of £150.

3.	The Jazz Café	Capacity 400	£2,000
4.	Dingwalls Dance Hall	Capacity 500	£2,500
5.	The Garage	Capacity 900	£3,500
6.	The Dominion Theatre	Capacity 1,900	£4,000 to £10,000
7.	Shepherd's Bush Empire	Capacity 2,000	£5,000 to £12,000
8.	Hammersmith Odeon	Capacity 3,400	£10,000 to £25,000
9.	The Royal Albert Hall	Capacity 5,600	£8,000 to £50,000
10.	Wembley Arena	Capacity 10,000	£25,000 to £100,000
11.	Wembley Stadium (RIP)	Capacity 74,000	£100,000 to £350,000
12.	Reading or V Festivals	Capacity 50,000 +	£500,000 plus
13.	Knebworth	Capacity 200,000	£1,000,000 plus

The above guesstimates are based on reasonable ticket prices. For the Albert Hall, I have shown the capacity as 5,400, but the actual capacity the promoter and artist have access to is only 3,800. This is because, when the venue was being built by Victoria as a memorial to her husband Albert, she persuaded 1,600 of her closest friends to put money into the work. For this contribution they received a seat for life and they could either sell their seat on or pass it down to their heirs. It is their heirs who today receive the income from those seats, and not as is usually the case, the artist and the promoter. It's one of the most beautiful venues for an artist to play – I cannot think of a more magnificent stage to walk onto. It's also a very artist – and audience – friendly venue.

Before we get bogged down too much on figures, let's just do one final costing here.

This one is so you can see how your fee comes out of the box office gross of one of the above venues. Let's take Hammersmith Odeon. I know it's now called the Apollo, but I can never get used to that after all the amazing Ry Cooder, Tom Waits, Jackson Browne, Undertones, Little Village, John Lee Hooker, Christy Moore, Van Morrison, James Taylor, Crosby Stills & Nash shows we did in the Hammersmith Odeon days.

1. COSTING FOR HAMMERSMITH.

Capacity: 3,400.
Ticket Price: £20.50, £18.50 & £16.50.
Gross Potential: £68,000.
Net Potential after VAT: £57,872.34

Running Costs:

Venue Rental:	£12,000.00
Performing Rights Society (3%):	1,736.17
Follow spot – rental & operators:	340.00
Ticket Printing:	200.00
Stage Manager:	200.00
Advertising, poster printing and distribution:	8,500.00
Artwork:	750.00
Security:	480.00
Venue Crew:	350.00
Stage Crew:	1,000.00
First Aid & Fireman:	70.00
Catering:	1,200.00
Public Liability Insurance:	99.00
Non-appearance Insurance:	360.00
Production Phone:	100.00
Towels:	14.40
Taxis (venue crew):	30.00
Gratuities:	80.00
Total expenses:	£27,509.57
Nett after expenses (amount left after deducting VAT and all expenses)	£30,362.77

Which means if your act was on £10,000 against 85% net, they will receive either a minimum of £10,000, or 85% of the net, whichever is the greater.

In our example above, 85% of the net is in fact £25,808.35. Which means the artist has more than doubled their guarantee, which kinda means that maybe the agent didn't pitch the fee as well as he, or she, should have. £20,000 would have been more on target!

So, on the above, the agent will receive 10% of the artist's fee, which works out at £2,580.83. And yes, the agency will invoice you for the 83 pence! All those 83 pences tend to come in handy, especially when you hear that one of the latter versions of NEMS agency ran into financial trouble when the bosses' secretary *filed* all the commission notes in her bottom drawer (not knowing what else to do with them), so for a considerable period of time no one sent out commission invoices to the artists. The oversight wasn't discovered until the secretary in question departed and someone took the trouble to go through her things!

The promoter will receive £4,554.42 for his trouble. However, if say the artist sold only half of the tickets, then the net after VAT would only be £28,936.17. This means after his expenses, which could drop to approximately £22,000, and the artist's fee of £10,000, the promoter is going to lose £3,063.83. The artist would *still* receive his fee of £10,000, and the agent would *still* receive his commission of £1,000 and the promoter would go boo, hoo, hoo all the way home!

So, promoting is a risky business, and if a promoter loses badly on a night (as is the case with the above scenario) it will take him two or three good nights to make it back again – a bit like gambling I suppose. A lot like gambling in fact.

But even gamblers like to minimise their risks, which brings to mind a development in the music business (particularly the *business* side of it) that you should be made aware of.

In recent times, the concert side of the music business in the USA and UK has been under a darkening cloud of the Clear Channel factor. An American company who owned a few radio stations in America, Clear Channel, started to buy up American concert promoters and American concert venues. They pretty much made a clean coast-to-coast sweep. With their new enlarged portfolio, they went back to their investors and raised more funds. With these funds they started to repeat the process in Europe. They bought out the major promoters in Holland, Sweden, Denmark, Switzerland, Belgium and several promoters operating in England. Again, as in America, they bought several UK venues too. The most recent development is that they have bought three UK agencies. All these were multi-million dollar deals. The problem I have with this situation is not where in the market place they are going to recoup their money, but more, in all of this, who is meant to be looking after the artist's interest?

You could, very easily, have a scenario in the UK where one company will own your concert promoter, your agency and the venue you perform in. In that instance I repeat my original question, who is going to be looking after the artist's interests? Clear Channel is trying really hard to become the only game in town. Now they are probably all very fine people who shake hands with old folks and kiss babies, but you have to wonder where it will stop? Will they want to buy publishing companies? Record companies? Newspapers? Television stations? I think the fear we all live under is that then they'll have the power to turn around and say to artists, here's the deal, it is the only deal in town, so like it or lump it. I hope I'm just being an alarmist and that these fine people are all music fans who care not for dividends and share prices but only for the songs.

*

Payment is a big issue and obviously an important issue. The golden rules with respect to money are:

> Never Pay to Play.
> Always collect your money in advance of the performance.
> When someone uses the words, "Don't you trust me?" run a mile.
> Have all payments made directly to yourself.
> Always sign your own cheques.
> Crisp Pink Grannies (£50 notes) don't bounce.
> Never do business with family members.
> Have a sign painted on your guitar case, "Please don't ask for credit, as refusal often offends."
> Make the deposit clause in your contracts "the essence" of your agreement, otherwise even when the promoter defaults he's entitled to his money back.

All the above are vitally important, but if I was to pick out the single most important two, they would be:

1. Have all payments made direct to yourself.
2. Always sign your own cheques.

One of the agent's main responsibilities is to protect the artist in the deal. Promoters can, and do, promote several artists but artists however have but one career and they (usually) have to gross a lifetime's earning in a relatively short career/earning period.

It's important, before you give the promoter the confirmation on the concert, that you have all your soldiers neatly lined up in a row. You have your faxes/letters and/or emails of the breakdown. There should be no mysteries, everyone should know, going into a deal, exactly what the terms and conditions are. There's *no* room or time for vagueness, or "I'll send you the information later, I need to get it up on sale as soon as possible," or the old Irish Showband promoter favourite, "Ah sure, we'll sort it all out on the night." Then when you try to collect, even your entitled fee, you'll get the speech about his mother's bankruptcy, his wife having run off with a farmer and taken his Merc, not to mention the fact that his mistress is so expensive. They'll paint the picture so bleak you'll feel so bad at taking any of your fee let alone returning the traditional luck penny.

So, when I ask (insist) on the promoter supplying costings (income and expenses breakdown), it's merely so the promoter and I can ascertain how much of the box office gross is left to be divided up between the artist and the promoter. Some promoters work under the misapprehension that if they pay the asking price (the guaranteed fee) they should be entitled to what is left. Their reality is that it's none of our business what the costings are. On the other hand, the artist and the agent's reality is that the guarantee is only the minimum fee the artist works for; the actual final payment is calculated as a percentage of the net box office figure.

Professional promoters will never enter discussions about whether or not they should be paying you a 50% deposit. They will never remind you how long you have known them and how long you have worked with them. Professional promoters will never guard the costings like they're a vital hand in a poker game. They know and respect the system. They are not in for a quick kill. Having said that, I'm sure that if it was offered to them on a plate they wouldn't turn up their noses at it.

You'll recognise a good promoter by the fact that he doesn't carry a box of Kleenex. Good promoters don't cry. Crying has become very popular in some areas of promoting circles over the last five years or so. Gone are the days when you can shake hands on a deal and that's it. That was all it took to cement the deal and both parties were happy to stick with it. Promoters used to be more considered about confirming their offers knowing that once they'd committed they were going to have to honour the deal. Nowadays, even some of the bigger promoters will offer anything you want – sometimes just to ensure that a rival promoter doesn't book the artist, or, at the very least, has to match his ridiculous offer to secure the deal – then they'll quickly stick the show(s) on sale and then come back crying if it doesn't sell out immediately. He'll want to either renegotiate or to cancel. I always remind each such promoter to think about how he would feel if I went to him after we'd confirmed the deal and said, "Sorry, but we're going to need more money."

No, the promoters who will waste time bartering with you over deposits and percentages are by and large the ones to be ignored. They're only in it for the quick buck. Pretty soon they'll discover there are few quick bucks available in the promoting game and they're off to their next little enterprise.

Yes, you see, trust is a fine thing and I admire it but it is never a word that people should hide behind and usually, when it's raised with you with regards to money you are due, alarm bells should start ringing in your head immediately.

10

THE FIRSTS

The first time things happen to you in this business it's very exciting and exhilarating. I think it's exactly the same feeling whether you're the artist, the agent or the manager. You know – milestone events like the excitement of your first mention in *Melody Maker* (RIP) or *NME*. In most instances, your first mention would be in the classified section and a single column wide, four cm deep, and it would have said something like "GOGGLES ANONYMOUS – semi pro band with org. material need drummer. No time wasters need apply. Ring Tony (guitarist) on Whitehall 1212." Yep, small, insignificant and nobody probably even noticed it except you and the people you tipped off. Drummers always seemed to be the hardest to find. It might be because most of them play with several groups, giving up on six when the seventh looks like it just might take off.

Drummers always seem to get the short end of the straw in the music business but there are also stories of more quick-witted drummers. Van Morrison had decided to take a rest from touring (or so the story goes) and he told his band that was it for a while. This particular drummer asked Van what he was planning to do in the down time. Van replied that he was thinking about making some documentary kinda films, and that he was looking for ideas on what kind of subject matter he might work with.

Quick as a flash the drummer chipped in, "I've got a great idea for one. Why don't you make a documentary about out of work drummers?"

Returning swiftly to your list of firsts, the next first will be when you see your name appear advertising your gig. Again, returning to the halcyon *Melody Maker* days, this usually meant you were opening for Brewers Droop at the Nag's Head in High Wycombe, but it didn't matter where you were playing or who you were supporting, you were *in* the club pages. The club pages were vitally important. So many times, when you rang up to get a gig, the venue bookers or managers would use the *Melody Maker* and *NME* Club pages as their bible. The more appearances you had, the more likely you would be to get a booking. The more bookings you've secured, the more you were in the club pages . . . the more you were in the club pages . . . I'm sure you get the picture.

Thin Lizzy (or Tin Lizzie if you were to use their pronunciation) worked out a very good short cut for this circuit. They went to several venues that ran on Friday and Saturday nights only, and persuaded the promoters to give them one of the other five free nights. The irresistible temptation for the promoter was that the band required no guarantee, just a straight percentage of the door. Then, having amassed 20 or so gigs, they persuaded their record company, Decca Records, to place small adverts, in the style of the venue's own adverts, in the club section of *MM* and *NME*. They had Decca repeat these adverts in the club pages week after week after week. Pretty soon, both the club owners and, more importantly, the audiences, wanted to see what this group, who were all over the club pages every week, was all about. Then Thin Lizzy released 'Whiskey In The Jar' and the rest is history, some of it happy and some of it sad.

In the clubs – places like The 76 Club in Burton-upon-Trent, the 1832 Club in Windsor, The Foxx at Croydon, Heads in Wimbledon, The Red Lion in Leytonstone – the rule of thumb was that you would play about three times as a support act and then you'd be given an opportunity to headline. Headlining was a major first. Of course we're talking here about a time when there was a healthy club circuit.

Getting your first encore was the next major first; only this one had knobs on. Generally this will be followed with your first wee write-up, usually in a local paper where you'd be mentioned in the main act's review. "Goggles Anonymous entertained a packed house until local sensation Brewer's Droop took the stage and worked everyone up into a frenzy blah, blah, blah . . ."

But at least you received your first mention, which was better than being ignored altogether. Well maybe not. Once people started to pay attention to you, they started to listen to you and (sometimes) that's when you wished that the press were still ignoring you, "With sloppy playing and pretentious material, Goggles Anonymous better watch themselves or they'll soon be in dire straits. Main act, Fruupp, however wooed the crowd with their magical material." That's not a quote from the *Fishmongers Gazette* in Grimsby, but it could have been.

113

You proceed through your firsts. First photo in the paper; first blowing off of the main act; first full write-up; first encounter with a groupie (always after your first write-up, *never* before); first record deal; first recording session; first record sleeve; first play on the radio (usually Radio Caroline at 3.33 am and you only hear half of the song because the weak signal keeps washing in and out, but you and the rest of their audience – seagulls – really enjoy it); first play on Radio One and then your wildest dream come true – your first chart entry.

Hallelujah! It's a big one this so I'll shout that again, Hallelujah!

Assuming your record company have been doing their work to ensure each and every chart shop (there are lists available) in the country has several copies of your single (mostly freebies) and that a wee bit of a buzz is starting and people are now going into the shops asking for, "Goggles Anonymous' new single, 'Sloop John C'" and maybe even some of them (like your families) will buy more than one copy, and the following Monday morning you hear that your single sold 457 copies and entered the chart at number 98!

Jubilation, celebration!! I really can't describe to you the joy that you'll feel achieving this wondrous milestone. You will feel such a rush that you'll literally be walking on air. You won't be able to sleep because you'll be so consumed by the fact that your first single has entered the UK pop charts!

The following week, the single climbs to 79. Your single has legs! The record company continues with their creative marketing – giving away more freebies to the chart return shops – and the week after that, your single drops to 80. Ooops! Misery, your first flop! But maybe not. The following week it climbs back up to 67. So it's back on track. Then, the week after, it jumps to number 42, missing the national chart (the Top 40) by just two places. The following week, the record company goes out and does its work properly and comprehensively. Your family, friends and relations go out and buy several more copies each. Your enemies return complimentary copies to the record stores.

Now, because you're a new act and bubbling under the charts, you will start to receive a certain amount of media attention. Here it will help greatly if you have a press hook your PR person can work on. You know, the sort of thing that sets you apart from the rest of the field. Things like the lead singer having a famous girlfriend – highly unlikely since you're not famous enough yet yourself – or one of the members of the band being related to one of the celebrity chefs – they're great for photo opportunities these days.

You'll be dreading and loving that Sunday Radio One *Countdown* show. When the DJ plays the number 40 record, you'll think, "Great, at least we didn't *just* make the 40." This thought will continue until you get to say the number 32 chart entry. Then you'll start to think, "Shit, we didn't make the Top 40 at all!" By the time the DJ gets to 30, you'll feel absolutely terrible. You'll be exhausted, wrecked, drained and you'll wonder why, because all you have been doing is sitting around listening to the radio. But the problem is that every second of the week you've just gone through will have been spent concentrating on the chart countdown, and now it's all over and you'll realise you're drained by the disappointment. You'll kick yourself for not doing that extra round of the special chart return shops in your area. (Check out *I Love The Sound of Breaking Glass* by yours truly for more on the art of chart hyping.) The masochistic part of you will force yourself to continue listening to the radio and then you'll hear, at number 29 the song that you hate by a group you know and last week their single was at 47, and here it is now at 29! That's why you'll hate the song; you'll hate them and their song in equal proportions because you'll feel they have stolen your opportunity.

You'd like to take the radio and shove it through the window but you can't, because all your family is sitting around you and they have all started to grow embarrassed by your failure to reach the charts. Your mother has probably already mentally spent her share of the royalties on a new suite of furniture for the living room. What share of royalties? Oh yes, she was going to speak to you about that at the appropriate moment. You'll be so mad that you probably won't hear the DJ announce, "And at 28, yet another new entry from a new group, this time it's Goggles Anonymous and 'Sloop John C'." Someone in the room will let out an embarrassing howl and there'll be several shouts and yelps. No matter how great the excitement, it will all sound a wee bit stifled, a wee bit stiff. The Americans are much better at this kind of stuff than we are; they are so much more uninhibited publicly than we are. Just look at the audiences in their game shows compared to ours. But anyway, the celebrations will continue around you, you'll be in a daze. Then you'll realise exactly what all the fuss was about when you hear the opening bars of your song being played on the national radio as the official number 28 best selling song in the country. It's a legitimate hit and things will never ever be the same again.

Savour these precious moments. From now onwards, every time this current single, and all future singles, moves up the pop charts, you'll feel okay, *just* okay. However if your current single drops you'll feel like Steve (Interesting) Davies, as in *totally* gutted. You have to ask the question: Why, if it feels so terrible when the single drops, does it not feel proportionally better when it moves up the chart? I don't know. All I can tell you is that it doesn't. And it's growing even more difficult in the current climate where the record company's rule of thumb is that if you don't make the Top 40 in the first week, you are *not* going to make the Top 40. Some 95% of current single releases peak in their first week! So in the vast majority of instances, it's all over in a week and you can't imagine how bad you are going to feel if that happens.

But the excitement we are talking about, you know, when you experience your first hit, well that is pretty much unbeatable, unless of course you achieve another (much rarer) first and your single takes over the coveted number one spot. Now that's an entirely different story altogether.

11

THE ROAD CREW

Most of the artists I know depend upon and trust their road crew more than they do anyone else they come into contact with in the music business. As I mention elsewhere, it's not unusual for Tom Jones not to act his age, no sorry, wrong tangent there – what I meant to say was that it's not unusual for one or several of the road crew to be with the artist right from the pub/club level up to the stadium level.

Jackson Browne's long-time manager and friend Donald "Buddha" Miller, started off as Jackson's roadie. He tells a great story of their early days on the road together when there was just the two of them; no manager, no other crew, and they'd play their way around America. Occasionally, they'd meet up with a promoter who'd want to take advantage of them by bumping them down the bill just because some other manager was out there hassling the poor promoter to push their particular act up the bill at Jackson's expense. It would either be that, or they'd want not to pay all the fee because . . . see separate list for poor ticket sales. So Buddha would always play dumb and say, "Gee, that sure sounds okay to us, but let me just ring the manager and see what he says."

So Buddha would pick up a pay phone backstage, as they were in those days, and dial a fictitious number and pretend to be on the phone to a phantom manager. Buddha would then repeat the request down the dead phone line and at the end of the request he'd go quiet and pretend he'd have to hold the phone a little away from his ear – obviously due to the screaming at the other end of the phone.

"Nagh, he's not that bad," Buddha would say into the mouth piece. "Oh erm let's see," then he'd put his hand over the mouth piece and say to the promoter, "He wants to know who you've got coming in over the next few weeks."

Buddha would repeat the list down the line and then say, "Nagh, I've told you, he seems reasonable to us, I don't think you'll need to do that." Or, "Nagh, I don't think that will be necessary."

Then he'd say to the promoter, "Well, we'd like to help you, I mean you've looked after us well since we arrived, but he's made it perfectly clear in no uncertain terms . . ."

And nine times out of 10 it would work, and they wouldn't be taken advantage of.

But by coming up through the ranks with Jackson, Buddha is perfectly placed to know how best to work the road and the road team to Jackson's advantage. He's learned first hand how effective the promoters, agents, local record company representatives, etc., etc. are, and he knows what he's dealing with, he knows how to deal with it. On top of which, he always puts together perfect teams of road crews.

Jackson often says that Buddha puts together the road crew with the same care and attention as *he* puts the band together.

Their production manager, Dennis Scrimo, is the perfect production manager in that he goes into all gigs with the approach, "Okay, what do we need to do to make the show work?" Some production managers seem to feel the need to flex their muscles by trying to evoke absolutely every clause on the contract to the letter.

Audiences benefit from Dennis' approach in that they *always* experience a beautifully produced show. And that's who we're doing all of this for; the audience. We want them to be turned on and go away having enjoyed their evening.

Never ever forget that it is the audience who keep us all in business.

I've met some tour managers and production managers who have bigger egos than their artists. They are right royal pains in the posterior and they make everyone's life a misery. I'd have to say that if there is a bad vibe backstage, it usually has a habit of finding its way into the audiences. Audiences are by nature acutely instinctive and pick up on a lot of this stuff subconsciously. They are sitting watching the artist and the artists seem to be playing all the right notes but there is just that little indefinable thing which is holding the members of the audience back and not allowing them to get lost in the music.

On the other hand, on one of the Van Morrison crews I discovered this astute Geordie called Alan Cranson. He was a bit like Radar in M★A★S★H in that he was always ahead of you, knowing what needed doing and no sooner would a musician start to say, "Alan I was wondering if you could . . ."

And he'd reply immediately, "Why aye man, I already dunnit," in his strong Geordie accent.

But the thing was that *every* single time he *had* already done it. It was quite freaky sometimes to be honest.

When Tanita Tikaram took to the road, we persuaded Alan to be her guitar technician and stage manager and since then any time she's appeared on stage, Alan Cranson is there as well. He's solid as a rock, very dependable. The important point I'm trying to get across here is that road crew like him are worth their weight in gold, because they give the artist the much needed sense of security. With their key crew in place the artist is fearless when they step out on a strange stage with strange equipment. The presence of people like Dennis Scrimo and Alan Cranson will give the artists the confidence they need to get up and concentrate on whatever it is they do on stage.

Mind you, I'd hate you to think that it was all rosy between crews on the road. There's always a bit of friendly competition and banter between the artist's road crew and some of the more, shall we say, white glove tour personnel. White glove crews are usually sound engineers or monitor engineers who don't get in with the equipment or get their hands dirty with the rest of the crew who are setting the gear up at the crack of dawn.

On one such tour the two crews had been . . . well not quite feuding for the whole tour, but pretty close. Anyway, the road crew is on a flight and the banter is continuing. The monitor engineer takes off his shoes to make himself more comfortable and the band's road crew eventually persuades him to go and blag a few beers from the air hostess. When he's away, and he seems to be away for an incredibly long time, the road crew spit in one of his shoes. Eventually the monitor engineer returns, they drink their beer, all the time winding each other up. Beers finished, one of the road crew says he'll go for another beer, but the monitor engineer insists he'll go and get them. Again, he's a long time away, and again they spit in his shoe, this time the other one.

Thirty minutes later, as they are getting ready to land, the monitor engineer slides his feet into his shoes, and the second he feels the dampness he says:

"You know what chaps, we're going to have to learn to get on better with each other, you know, all this spitting in each other's shoes and pissing in each other's beers is not really funny."

Being a roadie can also be dangerous at times. David Fowler was Dave Davies of The Kinks' guitar technician. Dave Davies does tend to play quite loudly and when the guitar amp is turned up loud, it's quite difficult to hear what's being said. One night Dave Davies was having trouble with his amp so he beckoned for David Fowler to come on stage.

Dave Davies was playing away and screaming at David Fowler and David Fowler couldn't make out a single word Dave Davies was trying to say. Dave Davies didn't want to interrupt the flow of the song, so he didn't want to stop playing his guitar just so David Fowler could hear what he was saying. Dave Davies had the idea to gesture with the neck of his guitar in the direction of the amp in the hope that David Fowler would get the clue that there was something wrong with his amp. Dave Davies swung his guitar in the direction of his amp and struck David Fowler smack in the side of his face and knocked him over.

David Fowler wasn't hurt too badly and a couple of the other roadies helped him off the stage and helped Dave Davies fix his amp.

The following night however, David Fowler had decided not to take any more chances and when Dave Davies looked over to him at the beginning of the set, he spied Fowler wearing a crash helmet!

*

You can see, even from just attending concerts, how the equipment side of things has developed and changed immensely over the years. From the primitive Public Address systems of the Fifties, to the high tech systems of today – where roadies with their soldering irons busy in the back of a speaker cabinet is a very rare, if not extinct, sight.

The development has been predominantly a road crew led one. It's been mostly road personnel who have, over the years, helped develop today's technology which is responsible for your favourite artists sounding as good on the stage of a venue near you as they do on the CD in your home. We're talking about radio microphones; on stage monitor systems; compact PA equipment; contact microphones for a grand piano; electronic pianos which sound just as good if not better than the real thing; foot-pedals which vary the guitarist's sound; projector screens; stage sets; on-stage monitor mixes; in ear monitors; travelling lights; vari lights; flight cases capable of securely transporting everything from delicate and sensitive equipment (and we're not talking about the guitarist!) to catering and wardrobe gear; even the front of house mixing system we now all know and admire.

The first artists I ever saw use this system were Crosby, Stills, Nash & Young at The Royal Albert Hall. Since those early days the front of house sound mixing desk has developed beyond all recognition. On the recent Jackson Browne Naked Ride Home tour they were using a Midas XL3 48 Channel Desk, which was so heavy, the local Italian road crew claimed they were not getting paid enough money to lift it. (Yeah, you're right, it always happens – or doesn't – in Italy.)

The Midas XL3 48 has 2,060 knobs to be turned, 3,168 buttons to be pushed, 74 faders to be slid and 62 magic eyes to be monitored. That's a total of 5,364 things to be done and if the sound engineer has to spend half a minute on each one of these manoeuvres in the course of a song, it works out at nearly 45 minutes to mix a four-minute song! Of course it's not like that at all. The skilled engineers – in Jackson Browne's case, Paul Dieter – set it all up in advance at the sound check and then just have to do a bit of fine-tuning when the audience comes in, and then a bit of tweaking for different songs.

So, let's talk about our roadies. Those fine men, and women, of the road who not only keep the wheels on the wagon but also return the rattles to the prams.

I worry about them. They are loyal to a fault. I think that I've already said, but it does bear repeating that without them this Playing Live circuit would grind swiftly to a noisy and unpleasant halt. But we are now beginning to have a situation where their part of the industry has crept into its fourth decade. So, if say you started your roadie-ing career in the Seventies, well you're now hitting the troublesome mid-Fifties, aren't you?

For instance, I list for you here 100 groups who had a career, but who, for one reason or another, didn't or couldn't make it last and provide their musicians and crew with a continued income: Fruupp, Quicksand, Quintessence, Principal Edwards Magic Theatre, Stray, Skin Alley, Head, Hands & Feet, Starry Eyed & Laughing, Gindlog, Magic Michael, Gypsy, Bakerloo Blues Line, The Spirit Of John Morgan, Caravan, Eire Apparent, Amon Duul II, Juicy Lucy, T2, Badger, Quatermass, Clark Hutchinson, Every Which Way, Camel, Help Yourself, Audience, Van De Graft Generator, Druid, Pink Fairies, Gong, Mighty Baby, Amazing Blondel, Quiver with or without The Sutherland Brothers, String Driven Thing, Edgar Broughton Band, Strackridge, Gentle Giant, Red Herring, Roogalator, Boxer, Iceberg, Man, The Motors, Climax Chicago Blues Band, Rare Bird, Capability Brown, Flash, Spiro Gyro, Bronco, Strider, Byzantium, Chochise, George Hatcher Band, Gentle Giant, Fat Mattress, Blodwyn Pig, Horslips, Radio Stars, Edgar Broughton Band, Babe Ruth, Skid Row,

Stud, Street Walkers, Medicine Head, Groundhogs, Trees, Hookfoot, Caravan, Hatfield & The North, Home, Trader Horne, Curved Air, Jackson's Heights, Balloons, Jack The Lad, East Of Eden, Trees, Atomic Rooster, Black Widow, High Tide, Steam Hammer, Writing On The Wall, Brush, Back Door, Alberto Y Los Trios, String Driven Dr Strangely Strange, The Enid, Cado Belle, Beggars Opera, Fumble, Hackensack, Daddy Long Legs, O Band, Nutz, Meal Ticket, Glencoe, Racing Cars, Sam Apple Pie, Trapeze, UFO and who could ever forget Wally!

Yes, there is at least one red herring in there, but there are also a hundred genuine gigging groups who were working on the circuit, playing to an audience and releasing albums. Fans were certainly supporting them, sadly though, not enough to ensure they could scrape a living out of it.

Some moved into management; some started their own service companies; some were wise enough to invest in property; some even got involved in stocks and shares. And you know what? Some even subscribed to pension plans. But the majority didn't.

Bands like The Who, though, did care about their crew and apparently always gave the proceeds from one gig on their American tours to their faithful team.

The majority of crews, though, didn't even notice their last 30 years on the road pass by; they were enjoying themselves so much. They have easily spent more time on the road with their artists than they have with their families. So what happens to them when they are no longer fit for the all-night drives, the early load-ins and the late load-outs?

You know what they say though, don't you? An old roadie never dies, it's always something he'll get around to doing, only later, once he's had a chance to check the band's gear just one final time.

12

THE ROAD

THE LOAD OUT

Jackson Browne
(by Jackson Browne & Bryan Garofalo, used by permission)

Now the seats are all empty
Let the roadies take the stage
Pack it up and tear it down
They're the first to come and last to leave
Working for that minimum wage
They'll set it up in another town
Tonight the people were so fine
They waited there in line
And when they got up on their feet they made the show
And that was sweet –
But I can hear the sound
Of slamming doors and folding chairs
And that's a sound they'll never know

Now roll them cases out and lift them amps
Haul them trusses down and get 'em up them ramps
'Cause when it comes to moving me
You guys are the champs
But when that last guitar's been packed away
You know that I still want to play
So just make sure you got it all set to go
Before you come for my piano

Playing Live

But the band's on the bus
And they're waiting to go
We've got to drive all night and do a show in Chicago
or Detroit, I don't know
We do so many shows in a row
And these towns all look the same
We just pass the time in our hotel rooms
And wander 'round backstage
Till those lights come up and we hear that crowd
And we remember why we came

Now we got country and western on the bus
R&B, we got disco in eight tracks and cassettes in stereo
We've got rural scenes & magazines
We've got truckers on the CB
We've got Richard Pryor on the video
We got time to think of the ones we love
While the miles roll away
But the only time that seems too short
Is the time that we get to play

People you've got the power over what we do
You can sit there and wait
Or you can pull us through
Come along, sing the song
You know you can't go wrong
'Cause when that morning sun comes beating down
You're going to wake up in your town
But we'll be scheduled to appear
A thousand miles away from here

STAY

Maurice Williams
new lyrics by Jackson Browne

People stay just a little bit longer
We want to play — just a little bit longer
Now the promoter don't mind
And the union don't mind
If we take a little time
And we leave it all behind and sing
One more song

(© 1977 Swallow Turn Music)

When artists are on the road they fall unconsciously into an on-the-road mode. The Jackson Browne song 'The Load Out' paints this picture very vividly. He really nailed it right on the head with those fine lyrics.

They live by their bible – their itinerary.

Artists, as you can guess, adore being on stage. It's the big treat and with a good audience, it's a celebration of the artist's work and equally of the audience's appreciation of that work. A great concert won't just be one where the artist rolls out all the old favourites. A great concert will be where magic is created between the artist and the audience; it is very much a two-way thing though. I think most people believe that a show is a bad show because the artist wasn't great on that particular night. And yes, sometimes that's certainly the case, but I've witnessed occasions where an audience, by their enthusiasm, will turn a potential average show into an amazing one.

When it works though, and artist and audience gel in this obviously tribal way, it's sheer magic.

And like all things magic, it's hard to capture or recall it accurately later. I've been to shows where the tears have been streaming down my cheeks and I'll be conscious of this being one of the best evenings of my life, yet the next day, when I go into the office, I can never find the words to convey just how special I felt the show was. It's not that in the cold light of day the feeling is betrayed or forgotten, it's just maybe more that it's been a very special moment but you need to have been in that moment yourself to realise just how special it was.

I've enjoyed many, but not countless, such experiences. Some, but by no means all, and, quite definitely, in no particular order, are:

Mary Margaret O'Hara @ The Dominion Theatre
Van Morrison @ The Rainbow Theatre
Genesis (with Peter Gabriel) @ Birmingham Hippodrome
Ry Cooder & The CS Band @ Dublin Stadium
Jackson Browne @ The Palladium, New York
Tom Waits @ The Dominion Theatre
Rockpile @ Loughborough University
Nick Lowe @ The London Palladium
Tanita Tikaram @ Musiccentrum, Utrecht
Ray Davies @ The London Palladium
The Undertones @ The Roundhouse, London
Bob Dylan @ Vicar Street, Dublin
The Blue Nile @ The Dominion Theatre
Loudon Wainwright III @ Dublin, Stadium
Tony Bennett @ The Royal Albert Hall
The Kinks @ Bilsen Festival, Belgium
George Harrison @ The Royal Albert Hall
Hothouse Flowers @ The Royal Albert Hall
Frank Sinatra @ The Royal Festival Hall
The Carpenters @ The London Palladium

I'm certainly a fan of records, I've been collecting them all my life but there's still something extraordinary about a live performance that you'll never ever get from a recording. The blend of their voices that evening for instance was so full and warm that they sent those old proverbial tingles down my spine. The words become more than lyrics, the music is more than an accompaniment. The live performance engages you more intensely than a recording ever can.

Take Mary Margaret O'Hara for instance. She has released but one album, the classic *Miss America*. It's one of my favourite albums of all time and it can be dangerous to listen to it with your eyes closed because it will take you somewhere you don't always want to go. But in her live performance you have no choice.

Mary Margaret, or M2OH as she's affectionately referred to on tour, is a good artist to talk about here because she probably demonstrates better than any other artist the effectiveness of the bush telegraph.

Her record was released first in North America and then in Canada. I read a review of it and immediately tracked down an import copy. Beautiful, magic, it was all the review said it would be plus more. I tracked M2OH down in Canada and persuaded her to come over for some shows. Virgin Records put out the album here and it got great press. People loved it, so by the time she came in to do her first show-case at The Venue, there was a full house waiting for her. Her live performance was so incredible we were able to bring her back a few months later and she sold out, in advance, the Dominion Theatre in London. That's 2,000 seats, near as, and all sold on word of mouth.

Sadly what M2OH does doesn't grow on trees, and she came back for only one further tour and has, to date, made no further recordings. She did visit the studio a couple of times, but told me that she felt that she found herself singing about the same things, albeit in a different way, and she didn't see the point in doing that. She said she found no satisfaction in repeating herself.

I think I've probably mentioned somewhere before but record companies, and even some artists, want you to buy each and every CD they ever release, whereas a fan's reality is that it makes them no less a fan of an artist if they only have say three of the artist's 10 albums. The same artists who are preoccupied with why album x hasn't sold as many as album y will also be the kind of artists who will play to empty seats.

What I mean is, they ignore the audience who are present because they are preoccupied with the people who haven't turned up, or who haven't bought their new records. I've seen this ruin a lot of concerts. So never play to the empty seats for fear there'll be a lot more empty seats next time. The same spoiler happens at a live show when an artist receives a bad review and feels they have to try and get their own back on the reviewer by reading out and ridiculing the review while on the concert stage.

M2OH wasn't capable of this; she's the real thing. When she goes on stage, she gives herself over to something bigger than all of this show business stuff. And it's the same with her record. So far, she's said all she wants or needs to say. I'll admit I'd love her to do a new album, but you know what, in the meantime, no matter how long that may be, I've got *Miss America* to listen to and the vivid memories of her magic concerts to enjoy.

But all of the shows I've listed above were for me times and places when a bit of magic was created and I was hugely privileged to have been present to witness and enjoy it. There's a different tale to tell with each one and a different set of memories to go with each concert; like

Blue Nile for instance. Peter Van Hooke – a good mate of mine and drummer and producer extraordinaire – and myself both went to see one of their rare performances. On this particular occasion, their show was at the Dominion Theatre in London. I wasn't their agent at that point and I'd never been to see them live before. Although I really enjoyed their two albums, I was in no way prepared for how much bigger their sound was live. It was massive, symphonic even, and very melodic. But there was more. There was Paul Buchanan's voice as well. He totally floored me the minute he started to sing. Paul Buchanan has a soulful voice that can move you as Otis Redding or Frank Sinatra or M2OH can and the show was just this amazing celebration of the band, their songs and Mr. Buchanan's voice. We left the theatre walking on air and floating above the forecourt of the Dominion after the first show trying to bribe people who were going in to the second show to sell their tickets. Eventually we bought a couple of tickets from touts and the second show wasn't better or worse than the first show, more like it was the second part of a performance.

And then there's the time I first visited NYC to try and secure a record deal for Fruupp – I almost did, it was all set up but then the keyboard player became a Jesus freak, I'll visit that later. Anyway I'd been a fan of Jackson Browne's music since the first album and have probably spent a good percentage of my life listening to his music – no particular album, all of them. But he'd never been to the UK at that point and then, during my NYC visit, I noticed that he was playing in the Palladium in New York for a couple of nights, two shows a night. As ever, all shows were sold out and so I went to the touts and used up all my remaining per diems to secure tickets to the shows. He was just magnificent, as anyone who's seen him play live will testify.

I believe all of the artists included in the list above are aware of the specialness of playing live and maybe this sensibility helps them catch these special moments. But, no matter how much these artists and all artists adore being on stage and no matter how magic it can get it's the remaining 21½ hours of the day that are the problem.

Some have easier times than others. Ry Cooder has, over the years, put on some really special shows. For a variety of reasons, not least dietary, he has never been particularly comfortable on the road. I remember on the single Little Village tour we found out that he'd been starving for three days while travelling around Europe because his wife's parcel of home-baked food hadn't arrived from the USA. Nick Lowe and I tried to do everything we could to get him to eat – to the extent of finding a friendly Indian Restaurant where the staff were not only happy to cook him a meal to his wishes, but also invited him to see them prepare the food. And he tried. Goodness he tried, he nearly got there, but in the end he just couldn't do it. Luckily enough, his wife's precious food parcel arrived the following day and disaster was averted.

There are many road stories, some funny, some, in reality, not so funny at the time but on reflection you've got to laugh. For instance, I remember Fruupp driving back from Guildford in our Ford transit van – nicknamed The Wasp due to its brown and yellow colours – and laughing our socks off as we spied a single wheel overtake us on the outside of the road. Our laughing soon stopped when we realised we were speeding along the road at a 20 degree angle and that what had overtaken us was our own wheel!

The Irish showbands generally travelled cramped up in the backs of vans as well and, as Ireland didn't enjoyed the motorway system of the mainland, the major showbands seemed to spend their entire life in the back of a mini bus. The musicians would have all their special seats and, in line with seniority, they would have their little perks. Like at the end of the night, usually anything from 3.00 am to dawn, when they would reach their home-town, the most senior members would be dropped off first, as sometimes the drop-off procedure could take an hour in itself. Derek Dean., was the lead singer of one of the best Showbands, The Freshmen, and it appears he was half-man/half-mattress in that he could sleep anyway, anyhow, anyplace, anytime. The story goes that they were all in the van in various degrees of alertness when Derek wakes up with a jolt and, not really knowing who he is, let alone where he is, shouts from his cramped position in the back, "Don't forget, I'm getting dropped off first."

"Whist, would you Derek," the driver replies impatiently. "Not only are we not on our way home; we haven't even done the gig yet, head."

Of course that was in the days before the magic word itinerary came into musicians' circulation. Nowadays the little booklet is literally what keeps all musicians and crew members on the same page.

*

Sharon Shannon, labelled by *The Times* as, "the Jimi Hendrix of the accordion", is an artist we've worked with for quite a time. She is truly a virtuoso musician and has a smile big enough to light up any venue she performs in. She and her fellow musicians always make the best of their time on the road where, as they say in Ireland, "The craic would be

90." A few years back when Catherine and I were getting married, we invited Sharon to play at the wedding. She graciously agreed to take time off from her touring to come to London for the wedding and it was duly marked up in her itinerary as:

"Sat 13 June 1999: Sharon and Jim only to London for P. Charles' wedding."

At around the same time, there were regular rumours in the press concerning a certain Camilla Parker Bowles and a, kind of, namesake of mine. While travelling to another of their concerts beforehand, Sharon's fiddle player was passing her time examining the itinerary in great detail, as you tend to do, and when she spied the June 13 entry she exclaimed to the rest of the tour bus:

"Shit, not only is the big wedding of Prince Charles and Camilla *on* but they've only gone and fecking booked Sharon to play at it!"

Anyway, Sharon did us proud on our big day. She had a lot of fans in the Donegal contingent, and I'd have to say if *that* other wedding ever does happen, the other P. Charles could certainly do a lot worse than to book Sharon Shannon to entertain his masses. Oh, and by the way, your Royal Highness, Asgard's telephone number is in the book.

Musicians do end up playing in the strangest of places and receiving the strangest of requests. Tom Waits and his family were on holiday in Ireland one summer and Tom took them all out for dinner to a special restaurant, to help celebrate the birthday of Kathleen (his wife and musical collaborator). They'd a great table; the food was excellent and just to round the evening off perfectly Tom slipped over to the restaurant piano and performed, by all accounts, one of the best versions ever of 'Happy Birthday To You'.

He was about to return to the family table, when the Maître d' came up and tapped him on the shoulder.

"Sir, we have had a request."

Tom obviously thought, "Oh here we go, I'm probably going to be playing here all night now, but it's my own fault, what the heck."

Tom looked up at the Maître d' and smiled an, "Okay."

"Yes, we've had a request from one of our patrons that you stop singing."

Luckily enough, Tom saw the funny side of it. I resist the urge to name the restaurant for fear that other customers would never darken their door again.

While on the road, you do get to visit some beautiful countries, see their finest cities and experience some amazing hotels, few more amazing than the Hotel Adlon in Berlin. This exquisite hotel, just opposite the Brandenburg Gate, one of the premier symbols of East Berlin, was built in the Twenties. The Nazis had hidden microphones in most rooms but the staff was cute enough to tip off the guests in the bugged suites. It's the same hotel where Louis B Mayer signed Greta Garbo to MGM and it was also the location for the filming of her famous movie, *Grand Hotel*. Sadly, the hotel was completely destroyed by fire just after the Second World War. Happily however Hotel Adlon was rebuilt and opened again in 1997. It's lobby is an incredible place to sit and have a coffee or a tea. If tea is your poison, you might want to try and ensure the staff heats the water right through to boiling point so you can enjoy a proper cup of tea. Their world-class Club Sandwich on the other hand is nothing short of perfection. The lobby is one of those places where you can enjoy all the entertainment you require by just hanging out. You can sit under the incredible stained-glass dome and unwind with a glass of wine while listening to the incidental music being played on the balcony above you. I'm sure few of the residents, visitors or guests in January 2002 would have realised that the music they may or may not have been tuning into for a couple of hours was being performed live by none other than the legendary Brian Wilson!

Brian was halfway through a very successful European tour, performing – with the help of an incredible 11-piece band – his famous album *Pet Sounds* in its entirety. Just for good measure he also did his audience the favour of throwing in a few of his other classics. While in Germany, the musicians were based in Berlin and staying at the Hotel Adlon. Come the early hours of one of the mornings Brian contacted his tour manager and enquired if the hotel would mind if he played the lobby piano for a while. The hotel is accommodating to a fault and of course they were cool with it. So Brian, unnoticed by the lounge lizards below, took up his position on the piano stool and proceeded to tickle the ivories. And what did his selection consist of? Beach Boy classics? Apparently not, this particular Beach Boy preferred instead to attempt the works of Rachmaninov, namely the Piano Concertos Nos. 1 & 3. I am reliably informed that he made a pretty good stab at them too.

Yes the road certainly produces its fair share of pleasures, although I'm sure some people just get so wrapped up in the old on-the-road-again game that they fail to notice a lot of the beauty they are passing through.

We did some shows with Lonnie Donegan, but he was such a glutton for working that he always had irons in various different fires. He'd ask you to do stuff, you know, like putting some gigs together for him which we would do, only to find someone else would be holding the same gigs for him. So I told him we couldn't work that way and we parted on good terms. A year or so later, he wrote me a nice letter saying he'd sorted out all his other stuff and he'd like to talk about us working together again on an exclusive basis. He wanted to know if I'd mind having a meeting with him to discuss his touring. I was a great admirer of his talent and I liked him very much as a human being, apart from which, he's a great story-teller, so I readily agreed and we put in a lunch for the following Monday. About 11 o'clock that morning, his wife, Sharon, rang up to say that Lonnie was a wee bit under the weather and would I mind if we post-poned the lunch. Of course not, I said.

Later in the afternoon I received another call, this time from Lonnie.

"Sorry about lunch, mate," he said.

"No problem, Lonnie," I said. "We'll do it another time. You sound terrible though, are you okay?"

"Actually, I'm in hospital, I came out from surgery about an hour ago."

"Oh! Listen Lonnie forget about all of this stuff, we can discuss it when you're feeling better. Now away off with you and rest," I said, finding it incredible that he'd be thinking about business so quickly after coming round after an operation.

It wasn't until the following day that I read in the newspapers that he'd had a quadruple bypass heart operation – his fourth I think – and he was still so desperate for work he was on the phone to an agent within an hour of coming round.

You see, he was part of the old school of show business where you always had to be working. Equally you always had to be *seen* to be working.

The last time I'd seen him was the previous year when he opened for Van Morrison in The Oxford Apollo. He was brilliant; he worked the audience like a trooper and had them all begging for an encore which never materialised due to the simple fact that the house lights came up before Lonnie even had a chance to get off the stage. It was a treat though to watch someone so in love with being on stage and so comfortable up there. In October and November 2002 some of his crew said it was unbelievable; he was like two different men on the road during what was to be his final tour. His last gig was in Nottingham, the city where, supposedly, he started his live career over half of a century before. Off stage he'd look tired, ill, weak, poorly and each and every one of his 71 years. But the minute he hit the boards, he was 10 foot tall and a teenager giving the show of his life again, just like he'd done every single night of his career.

Lonnie was a canny Scot, so he'd have known how to look after his money. On top of which, he'd written a few frequently covered songs like 'I'm Never Going To Fall In Love Again', as well as picking up the publishing on classics like 'Nights In White Satin' by The Moody Blues and 'A Whiter Shade Of Pale' by Procol Harum. So, you'd have to figure he wasn't fixing up meetings with an agent while on his sick bed just to pay for the weekly provisions.

That's the thing about artists like Lonnie. Health permitting, they never have an off-night, a bad night. It really is *in* their blood. They are true gigging musicians and I guess that means there also has to be a bit of a gypsy in them. You'd have to think that artists like Ray Charles, BB King and Bob Dylan have made enough dollars over their careers not to have to continue to live on the road. And the simple answer is that *yes* they have made enough money and yet they still do it, live on the road.

And they continue on the road playing live because they *want* to.

You see, Lonnie didn't start off doing this so he could still be on the road at 71 years of age putting up with hotels, airports, stage doors, musicians, crews, cars, buses, trains and bad weather; not to mention four heart bypass operations.

When you're on tour, you see, as Lonnie probably discovered early on in his career, something takes you over, takes over your life. When you wake up, you can feel you are connected to something, the pull of something, like a weak magnet whose strength grows as the day progresses. Your days disappear in a haze of hotels, buses, trains, fans, sound checks, food and autograph hunters – the professional kind a.k.a. "the uglies" because they care not about the music of the person whose signature they are after, they are merely chasing celebrities because they know the bigger the celebrity status of the owner of the squiggle they receive, the more money they will get for it when they sell it, which is what they will invariably do. All the time the magnet is growing stronger and stronger until it gets to the point where you no longer have the will to resist and then you step out on the stage and it all falls into place.

The magnet is the magic of the audience.

The second you step onto that stage, all your day will make sense. In an indefinable kind of way, you realise exactly why you want to do this. If the feeling was something you could put into words, it wouldn't have as much power over you and that's exactly the same for the artists and audience.

The great artists always look and behave comfortably on stage. They genuinely look like they were born to be up there. They are not scared of being on stage; they enjoy it immensely. Because of this, they are more likely to give a life-enriching performance, and not a recital.

The main difference between two seemingly talented tightrope walkers of equal ability is where one crosses the wire checking his fingernails while the other walks across respecting the distance between himself and the ground. The latter high wire artist learnt that showing off is not part of an act.

Similarly, a real artist will never feel the need to display his superiority vocally or on his chosen instrument. But at the same time, the consummate performer will be aware that his talent doesn't grow on trees and intuitively knows a performance is expected.

Celebrities, however, are a different matter altogether and have no place Playing Live. Check your local pantomimes for proof!

The true magic of playing live is that each and every night is a unique, never to be repeated experience, for both the band/artist and the audience. The magic gigs will stay in those people's hearts for the rest of their lives.

I still remember, as if it were yesterday, going to the Hammersmith Odeon to see Steve Harley & Cockney Rebel. It was in the Seventies and it was very nearly a religious experience. Steve has always made a special connection with his audience, it's like he involves the audience in the concert. He makes them a big part of the performance. Anyway, that night I remember leaving the Odeon with the rest of the 3,400 people in attendance and everyone singing:

> *"Oh look what they've done to the blues the blues,*
> *oh but it's magic, the best years of their lives."*

The audience continued singing this in the street as they broke up and went their separate routes, breaking down into smaller and smaller groups but all the time continuing to sing the lines. It was definitely magic, but you had to have been there.

So, I suppose what I'm saying is that when you have the opportunity to experience a great artist playing live, you'll get to experience magic being created right there before your very eyes and ears and you'll go home with your heart and soul warmed by the artist.

I wanted to top and tail this chapter with the lyrics of two fine road songs, the second of which is Loudon's 'The Home Stretch' but it was a toss-up between this and 'Motel Blues', another all-time classic road song from LW3.

THE HOME STRETCH

Loudon Wainwright III

If the day off doesn't get you
The bad reviewer does
At least you've been a has-been
Not just a never was
And you know it's not a mountain
But no mole hill is this big
And you promise to quit drinking
As you light another cig

Once again you're in the home stretch
But you're not sure where you live
You recall a small apartment
And a government you give
Large amounts of money to
So you're allowed to stay
And rest until you're well enough
To leave again and play

You are making human contact
With the postcards that you send
To the children of your ex wives
And a woman, your girlfriend
Who is living in a city
Thousands of miles away
That's full of male models
Not all of whom are gay

Too many beds, too many towns
Not much to declare zones
London boils and tuna melts
On dirty microphones
While the sound man's fallen fast asleep
The lighting man's been up for days
The club owner and arithmetic
Have long since parted ways

135

Playing Live

As for your lovely audience
Tonight they're rather cold
But they're prepared to listen
All they have to do is be told
If the day off doesn't get you
Then the bad reviewer does
At least you've been a has-been
And not just a never was.

13

THE PROMOTER

Wanted: Customers
(Sign outside a Camden Town pub)

PART ONE – PROMOTING THE SHOW

That simple chalk written sign shows that the proprietor is aware that he has to promote his venue. It's pretty basic; it's pretty simple. It doesn't matter if you're looking to fill your pub with drinkers, or you're trying to sell out Knebworth with paying fans, you have to get out there on the street and promote your event.

That may sound like the single most obvious thing for me to have said in this book. But sadly, it's perhaps the most necessary thing to have said. Chris Blackwell, or one of his Island Records' team, once produced a beautiful full-colour poster, which in effect said:

IF YOU DON'T PROMOTE
A TERRIBLE THING HAPPENS.

NOTHING!

I still have a copy of this poster and I hope I always will.

You see some promoters don't actually promote. They are producers; they are ticket sellers, yes, but they couldn't promote their way out of a paper bag. Anyone can put on a concert with Paul McCartney, announce the concert details and sit back and watch the tickets sell. But a good promoter, or even a great promoter, can take an act, an unknown act, and just by virtue of the fact that the act we are talking about are great, can go out and help find an audience for them.

It's a lot like the dating game really, this promoting business. You know, they say when looking for someone it's best that you find someone . . . who is looking. Well most of the people I know are continuously on the lookout for good music and it is my belief that there are a whole tribe of like-minded people in this and most countries.

So let's examine exactly what a promoter does.

First off, he has to do a deal with the agent. Again, back in Chapter Nine, you will see a set of figures for a concert in Hammersmith. There's also a separate guesstimate figure as to what artists can take out of the various venues as a fee. Promoter and agent will haggle in time-honoured fashion and an agreement will be reached. If the agent is a great agent, he will not necessarily give his act to the promoter who offers the most money. Most of the promoters who have been in business a few years think they know how to do this promoting malarkey. The two things to be assured of by your promoter are:

- **That the promoter has a personal commitment and belief in the artist.**

This belief in the artist will be necessary to encourage the promoter to invest his time, energy and money in the artist. Not every artist who comes along is going to be successful in the commercial sense of the word. What this means is that some of the artists who come along are going to lose promoters (and record companies) money. So, in effect, what promoters are doing is gambling their money on the fact that so and so, say for instance Goggles Anonymous, are going to be successful long term, and that they are going to make back their initial investment before either the artists in question split up, or move on to work with another promoter.

Like professional gamblers, professional promoters will have the knowledge, their gut instinct and the access to information on which they rely in order to minimise their risk. But really, at the end of the day, it does come down to the fact that they are taking a punt.

- **That the promoter can activate the bush telegraph.**

Every town has a very effective bush telegraph for new artists. There are a group of journalists, disc jockeys – usually late night – independent record shop owners and social secretaries who love nothing more than being turned on to great new music and, in turn, be responsible for turning the audience onto it. It's all meant to be very sophisticated, but basically it's still pretty much like it was back in the old school playground where major credit points are dished out to the first kid on the block to introduce such and such.

Initially, it's no use placing an advert saying Goggles Anonymous are going to appear at, say, Dingwalls in Camden Town. No use whatsoever. Obviously at this stage in their career, no one even knows their name, so there is a very good chance that 99.9% of readers won't even register the advert, let alone take in the details. This is a mistake many of the bigger producer/promoters make. They think that by just taking out lots of adverts, printing and sticking up posters, printing and distributing leaflets, it'll be fine, our magic audience will turn up out of the blue and we'll all live happily ever after.

These are the same promoters who are on the phone to the agent with the line, "We've run the figures through the computer and we've worked out at the current rate of progress" – say for argument's sake zero – "we are going to sell a minus figure" – it may sound stupid but their programme will have a proviso to include an amount for ticket returns – "and so the show is cancelled."

It's a sign of the times I'm afraid. In the good old days, a promoter's word was indeed their bond, like with the aforementioned Gentleman Jim Aiken. In fact the reason I mention Jim Aiken here again is because with Jim, you knew not only that when he gave his word you were covered better than any contract would ever have covered you, but also, and more importantly, he and his team would still give the Rolls Royce treatment to the artist, whether the house was packed to the rafters or it was empty, and he was losing his proverbial shirt.

Okay, spending money is not enough, so what do you do to find your audience? Well, it's simple really. What you have to do is to put music to the name. You have to make sure that when someone comes across the name Goggles Anonymous, they stop and think, "Oh yes, they're the great bespectacled group with the amazing guitarist, or singer, or songwriter, that sounded incredible on *The Robert Elms Show* and I really do want to go and see them." It can be Robert Elms, Charlie Gillet, Johnny Walker, Bob Harris or Jonathan Ross. They're all on the radio and they're all great about playing new music and giving people live sessions.

Next there are a bunch of journalists who are equally supportive and, assuming they like the music, they'll do a write-up in the newspaper. Then you either stick the act on a showcase show or as an opener for an established act. Again you'll usually find the same journalists, disc jockeys, or their producers, in attendance and they'll go off and review and report how great the show was.

So now you are on the top deck of the number 159 red classic Routemaster bus on your way to work and you spot this eye-catching poster. It's a gynormous pair of spectacles. You are reading *Time Out* a few seconds later and you see the same image in an advert. A few pages later you see a great preview from Jim Driver. On the way into work you go into Rhythm Records near Camden Lock to buy tickets to see Ocean Colour Scene at The Electric Ballroom, and you spot the Goggles Anonymous leaflet on the counter. You read the leaflet carefully, mainly to escape the attention of the guy standing next to you who is using the counter as a phantom keyboard to finger the chords of the ELP track being played on the store sound system. Then you remember *The Robert Elms Show* and how great Goggles Anonymous were on that and you decide to go to Dingwalls Dancehall to see the band. Of course it's not quite as simple as that, but sometimes it actually is.

The part about promoting I enjoy most is producing the artwork for the poster, adverts and leaflets. Okay, let's take time out here again for a little test. Do you remember your journey into work this morning (assuming you are not an out of work musician of course)? Do you remember any of the poster sites? Do you remember any of the posters? Do you remember any of the artists mentioned on any of the posters?

Same with the adverts in *Time Out*, or any other magazines, do you remember any of the actual adverts? Of course we, the promoters, agents, managers, record company people, etc., do, because we're looking out for them. But the general public, our target audience, usually flick through the adverts to get to an article or to a review or whatever. On the street we're more likely to be distracted by the glimpse of a beautiful †young lady, †man, †girl or †boy (†delete to taste) walking by, than we are picking up all the small print on a poster for the split second it is in our vision.

I like to try and come up with visuals that will turn people's heads, will make them stop and pay attention (hopefully). You can do this in two ways: by creating an event and you can do it with your artwork.

We once promoted Elvis Costello & The Attractions for five nights at The Hammersmith Palais. However, to give it a bit of a twist, we agreed with his manager Jake Riviera that Elvis would play every consecutive Monday night for a month. Luckily enough, there were five Mondays in that particular October. At that time, Elvis was capable of selling out a couple of nights at Wembley. I don't care what anyone says, I think Wembley is a terrible place for music and once you're done you're done, thank you and goodnight, next please. But with the five Mondays at the world famous Palais you have five different chances to get the media down. On top of which everyone likes a change, and the media are always on the lookout for a different story to tell. Okay, so we have our unique event, now all we needed to do was to get the public's attention.

Let's just return to my point that it's easy to ignore adverts and posters. So, what can we do to catch people's attention? I figured Elvis fans are more concerned about hearing about their idol's shows than they are with seeing flowery artwork. So, the hook is obviously the name ELVIS COSTELLO. We need to make that jump out. So we did. We printed a very long poster, three times the normal length in fact, and made up in three parts, with Elvis Costello in very large letters, gold on a black background, going the whole way across the posters. When this set of posters went up on the London poster sites, it literally jumped out from all the other posters and demanded your attention. Basically they were so in your face they were impossible to ignore. We did the same thing with the adverts. Instead of taking a quarter page, half page or full page as is the norm we took a six inch strip, but continued it across two pages so that we would have maximum impact. We had the artwork done so that the letters looked like they were too big for the advert, spilling off the edge of the space. When people opened the relevant pages, ELVIS COSTELLO (the name) literally jumped out at them and then, those who were interested, read the additional details to find out when, where and how.

The campaign worked a treat and the tickets for the five nights sold out in less than an hour!

Obviously the other part of promoting a show is with the artists participation. Most artists make themselves generally available for interviews to help promote their own shows in person. Personally speaking, I'm not sure whether they are being persuaded to make themselves too available. More importantly, I'm not sure fans want to see their artist appear on breakfast television or being interviewed in depth in the *Hull Fishmongers Gazette*. Apart from anything else, there are only so many ways you can tell the same story or make the same pitch. Again, the plot seems to have been somewhat lost. Interviews are not meant to be a series of plugs. They are meant to be opportunities for fans to be enlightened about their artist. I'm sure 95% of music fans (yet again another music business statistic made up on the spot) would prefer a ten page *Mojo* interview, than the quick quarter page fix they are being offered in numerous mags all stating the same thing. Namely:

1. I have a new album out.
2. I am touring in your neighbourhhood shortly.
3. Some unshaven trendy has done a remix on my new single.
4. We shouldn't have gone to war with Iraq.

People like Bob Dylan and Van Morrison don't get mixed up in this shit and yet they still seem to sell a fair number of tickets and records.

Less is more. I'm sure everyone's interests would be best served with one comprehensive interview in *Mojo*, *Uncut* or *Music* and a smaller one in one of the quality dailies. This would allow the artist to save their energy for radio and television and concerts. You see, on radio, television and the stage there is nothing that can come between the artist's music and the audience. As long as Goggles Anonymous are in a position where they are allowed to air their music, they can't really go wrong. But the major problem is that this is now an industry, the media is also now an industry and they are both parts of the larger entertainment industry. The entertainment industry is a ugly big fecker of a machine that needs to be fed continuously. The machine has a preference for new blood and legendary names and it will tolerate the remaining 80% in between in return for the favour of the new blood and the legendary names.

And wouldn't you know that the less the new blood and the legendary names want to do this stuff the more they are sought.

Sometimes it destroys you and that's equally true if you do too much or do too little.

Take The Roches for instance. The Roches were three sisters from NYC who were the toast of that particular town. So much so in fact that the record companies came calling. Mr. Warner and his brothers signed them up for a seven-album deal. They recorded a wonderful debut album, The Roches, with engaging, melodic and superbly crafted songs. The industry goes ga ga on them. They're going to be the next Joni Mitchell – which I personally found weird, I always thought Joni Mitchell was a solo artist – the next Paul Simon, the next Kate & Anna McGarrigle, the old Be Good Tanyas or the last Indigo Girls. To me, they were always purely and simply the The Roches. Their shows were just amazing: wacky, emotional, comical, therapeutic, hypnotic and so downright honest. They received the reviews of a lifetime. They made front pages here, there and just about everywhere. People wanted them to do *Saturday Night Live*, to support Bon Jovi (!!!), record with Ted Templeman, go here, do this, do that. (That's just the printable version of the list.)

And the three sisters just freaked.

They didn't have a manager, which didn't help matters, and they were suspicious of everyone chasing them offering them stuff to do, stuff they simply *must* do. Their built-in self-protection mechanism kicked into gear, with the direct result that they just started to say, "No!" to absolutely everything offered to them. They figured that would be the safest way to protect their sanity. They spent time letting things calm down, regrouped, got their heads together and started to contact people to say that now they were ready to do this seriously. And guess what? They discovered that in a matter of months, they were, sadly, already seen as "last year's thing". Nicolette Larson and Dire Straits had moved up to become Warner Bros' new kids on the block.

The Roches had missed their chance, big time.

And even then when you do every single thing you're asked to do, it doesn't necessarily mean everything is going to work out fine. We'll see from the following example that there's just as big a problem when some of your work becomes too successful.

We worked with Dexy's Midnight Runners. We took them on in the third week of their eight-week stay at the top of the UK charts with 'Come On Eileen'.

Dexy's didn't have a hit single in America, and yet 'Come On Eileen' was the number one single for eight weeks in the US charts.

Confused?

Here let me explain. Dexy's promoted the heck out of that single and did every single thing asked of them. The single also topped the US charts for a very respectable eight weeks, starting in January 1983. I had booked an American tour for them that started on the sixth week of that run. The first show was in Boston, and guess what? A pathetic 87 tickets were sold. Next stop Chicago wasn't much better with ticket sales in the early hundreds, and on and on it went and then, after a while, I realised despite the fact that all of America, or at least the 1,000,000 who'd bought the song, knew 'Come On Eileen' very well, little or no one equated the single to, or with, Dexy's Midnight Runners.

I learned the hard way that a million-selling single can in fact hurt your career. Other examples would be 'Dance The Night Away', which was the death knock for The Mavericks and 'La Bamba' certainly hammered at least one nail in Los Lobos' coffin. All three, up to the point of their mega hit single, were seriously credible groups. All of that credibility went out the window as fast as they climbed the charts. You see when you enjoy that illustrious number one single, although it certainly does wonders for your credit rating (as opposed to bank balance), the more critical sections of the media tend to file you as lightweight. That's all very well if you've already made the cut, but if you haven't, the press are not going to be there for you when you need them most. Dexy's only other US chart entry? 'The Celtic Soul Brothers', which was the follow-up to 'Eileen' and reached the giddy heights of number 86.

Having said that though, one valuable tip I've discovered is never to use the word "No" to your record company.

That doesn't necessarily mean you should say yes to every single thing they request you to do. But you have to realise that most of your record company staff also have an ego, sometimes bigger than the artists they are working with, so when you say "No" to one of their ideas/requests/suggestions they're likely to say, as they set the phone down, "Feck you. You're finished, there are plenty of others who'll be glad of the chance."

So, instead of that little two letter negative retort, try, "Well I'm not sure that would work for us. It's a good idea and I can see where you're coming from, but why don't we . . ." and then hit them with a counter-proposal, which you allow to become *their* idea.

As they say in the Tin Pan Alley Ghost Town, "Success has many fathers, but failure is a fatherless child." (That's the polite version of the quote, mind you, I could never figure out how a bar steward fitted into the other version.)

The final illustration in this section about methods of promoting yourself and your tickets could probably be filed under the heading, "Be careful how you behave on the way up and you just might miss the sharpened swords on the way down."

The Cranberries versus The Corrs syndrome: you may remember that the lovely Dolores from The Cranberries used her interview platform to be, shall we say, less than positive about The Corrs. The Corrs, as far as I am aware, refused to rise to the bait. They were professional in their dealings with the press and did what professional musicians do, talk about their music. They worked hard, they did all of what was asked of them and they got on with the job in hand, which was creating and promoting their music, wisely choosing to keep their non-musical views to themselves. Meanwhile Dolores gained a reputation for being a "diffi-cult" interviewee and, indeed, spent quite a bit of her airtime making public her distaste for the media.

Everything was fine when The Cranberries were selling millions of albums, but then came the time for the media to get their own back by suggesting that their new album wasn't as good as their first two classics. The critics had the long knives well sharpened and they quite literally killed the album dead on its release date. And if that wasn't enough, the newspapers brought up the old competition thing between The Corrs and The Cranberries in all the interviews the lovely Dolores undertook to try and breathe some life into her album campaign. Yet again she rose to the bait on The Corrs. The Corrs *still* refused to get involved and sailed on, heads held high. A few days later it was all over the Irish papers that The Corrs' new album (released the same week) cruised straight to the coveted number one spot, whereas The Cranberries *strug-gled* to reach number nine.

Now it's all in the telling of the story, isn't it? Who in their right mind wouldn't give their eye-teeth for their new album to go straight into the Top 10 of the UK Charts? The problem is that the majority of artists never ever look at who is below them in the charts, paying atten-tion only to those in the loftier positions.

I suppose another translation on the above could be, "Make sure your criticism is sweet; you may have to eat it yourself someday."

Promotion is, in a way, very relevant to the times. For instance, in the Sixties The Love Affair were arrested and, I believe, prosecuted because as a promotional exercise they had their photograph taken atop one of the lion statues in Trafalgar Square. Right, now think of The Sex Pistols and some of their promotional activities in the Seventies. I bet if the Pistols had been around in the Sixties they'd have been beheaded.

Another extreme of promotion is when it's too successful an exercise.

Take Dire Straits for example. It's been alleged that Mark Knopfler was so concerned about the lack of commitment from the audience attending Dire Straits' concerts following the phenomenal success of *Brothers In Arms*, that he had discussions with his record company about trying to get some of the records back again.

Time for just a little story here to illustrate exactly how big Dire Straits were.

In the early Eighties Dire Straits were indeed mega absolutely every-where, but particularly in Italy. *Making Movies*, their third album was number one there for something like 28 weeks. It sold 700,000 copies and the demand for the band to visit for concerts was phenomenal. They, like the majority of big bands, were reluctant to tour Italy because of Communist led riots at gigs there in the Seventies.

The Communist philosophy was that music should be free for everyone, so they would gather together outside gigs in their thousands, literally, and break their way in by rushing the doors, windows, roofs, anything that was penetrable. The result was that there were riots at most gigs and on more than one occasion the artists' equipment was totally destroyed in the process.

Following lots of pleading, requests, demands, Ed Bicknell and Dire Straits eventually agreed that they would play some Italian shows. Ed cleverly rid himself of the competitiveness and in-fighting between all the promoters by making the top three promoters partners on the Dire Straits' shows. They agreed to do five shows in stadiums. Each stadium would have a maximum capacity of 30,000. When he received the itinerary through from the three promoters, he was surprised to see that all five venues were called Stadium Communal. The first four gigs were relatively problem free but when they arrived at Turin, the final gig on the tour, to do the sound check, their driver pulled up, with Ed and Band in the back, at the Juventas football stadium. Ed laughed. He pointed to the itinerary and said, "Stadium Communal, Stadium Communal."

"Si, Si," the driver said, pointing to the rather large football stadium.

"No, no," Ed replied and found what he was looking for.

Behind the main stadium, he spied a much smaller run-down stadium, which was obviously the footballers' training ground and much closer to the 30,000 capacity he'd been expecting.

The driver reluctantly agreed to drive them over to it.

When they reached the smaller stadium and entered, there was no stage, no crew and no equipment.

The driver kept pointing to the main stadium, "Si, si, musiak, la, la, la."

So they all jumped back in the car and drove across to the main stadium again where, right enough, they found their crew, who looked like they were about a tenth of an inch tall, putting up their equipment on what looked like a matchbox. Their equipment looked tiny and was dwarfed out off all proportion by the size of the venue. During the sound check, there were 3,000 people sitting in front of the stage watching the band rehearse. The crew was told that they were the families of the security and had to be allowed in for free. The doors were opened at 15.00 and people began arriving. Then some more arrived, and some more and then still

146

some more. At about 19.00 John Illsley came to Ed and told him that he didn't want to worry him, what with all the other problems the manager was having, but that people were actually streaming through the band's dressing room windows by the thousands. Just before Dire Straits were due to go on stage, the security took off their fluorescent jackets and, abracadabra, became members of the audience. Anyway, at 21.30 the band went on and had a great evening.

After the concert the promoter and his accountant took the band and Ed out after the show to savour one of the true joys of touring Italy, a dinner, over which the figures for the evening's concert were to be finalised.

The accountant stated that there were 37,280 in the venue.

Laughs all around.

"But it was packed; you couldn't possibly have gotten another single person in the stadium."

"I know," the promoter replied proudly, "37,280 people!"

"But when Juventas play a football match there they have 80,000!" Ed protested.

"Yes, but of course."

"Well, we had a full house *plus* the football pitch was covered in people as well."

"Yes," the promoter agreed not considering the mathematical implications, "we had 37,280 people."

Ed was considering the magnitude of the blatant deception when the accountant proudly produced a piece of paper from his inside pocket.

"There were 37,280 people in the stadium," he claimed flamboyantly, "and I have a government certificate to prove it!"

Ed was too long in the tooth to get bogged down with squabbling. He knew and agreed with Col Tom Parker's famous quote, "If a promoter wants to f**k you, there's nothing you can do to stop them."

The secret is to protect yourself as much as you can at the top end. Your other protection is that you just don't work with the promoter next time around.

Ed and the band sat back and started to enjoy their meal.

But there's more.

After the first course, the accountant passed out, his face falling straight into his food. Apparently he was also a drug dealer who liked to sample his goods a bit too much. The promoter ordered an ambulance and took his accountant to hospital, returning shortly thereafter with the immortal words:

"So, he's dead. Now let's finish our meal!'

And there's even more. Guess how many t-shirts the band's official merchandisers sold to the 87,000 odd people in attendance that night?

Okay I'll tell you – 22! And the reason wasn't the band's dwindling popularity. They were still a long way from the *Brothers In Arms* peak. The reason was that the bootleg mechandisers had set up their own wagon train round the venue and were doing a roaring trade with their own illegal stuff. Illegal bootleggers are a common occurrence with the big bands around Europe. It gets to be an even bigger joke when the band sends out their road crew to pick up some of the illegal swag because it's usually such great swag.

"Why are the bootleggers designs always better than ours?" Mark Knopfler asked his manager on one such occasion.

"Easy," Ed replied, "because they don't have to get you to approve their artwork!"

Jon Landau once rang Ed saying that his client, Bruce Springsteen, was interested in playing in Italy. Ed laughed for minutes and then said, if you go don't expect your rider to be honoured, don't expect the gigs to be where they said they were going to be, don't expect a proper stage, don't expect proper accounting, you'll be fine . . . if you do go expect strikes in the middle of the gigs, riots in the middle of the gigs, expect your gigs will be taped and bootlegged before you even get a chance to leave the country, expect to see beautiful women, enjoy great food and wonderful towns and cities and you'll have a grand old time.

Four months later, Jon Landau rang Ed back, thanking him and saying, yes, the food had been wonderful.

PART TWO – PRODUCING THE SHOW

When Ed Bicknell started off his career as a social secretary, the art of producing a show was a lot simpler than it is today.

During his two-year tenure at Hull University, Ed promoted 50 shows. On none of those nights did a band turn up with more than two crew – except that is The Who, who had "two and a half". It's the way Ed tells them! On top of which no act arrived before 7.00 pm for an 8.15 show, they all did two sets of 45 minutes each; all that was except for The Moody Blues whose bass player John Lodge sought out Ed to advise him: "We don't do that two-set show any more. We only do a 75-minute *concert* now. People sit down and listen to us."

"No way," said Ed. "It's Saturday night at the student's union, they're only interested in girls and alcohol. They're not going to sit down and listen to anyone."

But the students of Hull University did sit down on the floor and listen to the Moodies perform their *Days Of Future Past* album in its entirety. The Moody Blues had another strange request that night. They were on a fee of £100 and the contract said, "Cheque to office". The band's lead vocalist, lead guitarist and, obviously, lead spokesman, Justin Hayward, claimed they would never see the fee if it went via the office and so asked Ed for cash. He paid them £90 cash and sent the balance to the office.

As an aside to an aside, the Moodies came across their unique sound by accident. They'd been in search of a Hammond B3 Organ and they'd seen one advertised in a Midlands Working Men's Club for £50. A bargain. Money changed hands, the Hammond was picked up but when it was set up in the Moodies' rehearsal studio, keyboard player Mike Pinder asked where the Leslie Cabinet was. The Leslie Cabinet gives the Hammond its unique sound. Mr. Pinder was duly informed that there wasn't one. He soon discovered that there wasn't a Hammond either. It turned out that the Moodies, like the Working Men's Club before them, had bought a Mellotron sight unseen, as it were, and so the Moodies unique sound and success was set in motion.

As a social secretary Ed booked bands like Pink Floyd, Led Zeppelin, The Moody Blues and Jethro Tull. The Tull were number one that week with *Living In The Past* and appeared for a £400 fee. No artists, even those on a percentage, would ask what the ticket price was? Nor would they enquire on the exact capacity, or if indeed they had broken percentage. One of the local groups continually blagged Ed for support spots. They were called The Rats who later became The Spiders From Mars.

That was when 7.00 pm was sufficient time for the equipment to be set up. Now the get-in is closer to 7.00 am and promoter and social secretaries no longer *book* their *shows*. No – thanks in no small way to the Moodies and similar groups with their preference for their "in concert" approach, they, promoters and social secs now *produce concerts*!

And what does this producing entail?

When the promoter is enjoying the 33rd of his nightly 40 winks, his rep, or production manager, along with an eight to 20 man team of local road crew (humpers) will be unloading the artist's several articulated lorries. These 40-foot trailers are jam-packed with the artist's PA system, lighting system, backline, stage sets, catering system and merchandising, all neatly and safely packed away in roadworthy, if not indestructible, flight cases. By the time the last of the flight cases have been wheeled to their predetermined position the artist's road crew will arrive and proceed to start to set up the equipment.

The artist's crew comes in four tiers:

1. The tour manager, production manager and stage manager. Depending on the stature of the artist these three responsibilities can be undertaken by one, two or three people.
2. The sound engineer, the monitor engineer and the lighting operator. The sound engineer controls what the audience hears, the monitor engineer controls what the band hears on stage and the lighting operator paints the pretty patterns, hopefully enhancing, and not distracting from, the music.
3. The artist's long serving travelling stage crew, including guitar techs, keyboard techs and drum roadie. In many instances some, if not all, of this set will be mates of the band.
4. The crew who come with the tour suppliers (PA, lights, stage sets, buses, trucks).

The production manager and stage manager do a fair percentage of their work in advance, so, by the time they arrive at each venue there should be neither mysteries nor problems. The crew will all go about their jobs efficiently and expertly. The band's crew usually shares in-jokes and road stories with the local and suppliers' crews. Road crews are always talking. The band's immediate crew work exclusively and full time. They are with each other year in and year out and still you'll find them chatting and joking away as though they were long-lost friends who'd just met up again after years apart. They are fiercely loyal to each other and to their act. In the same way you will find a band has a distinctive look, you'll also find that crews sometimes share a similar look. This is usually because of the free SWAG the crew collects as they travel from country to country, picking up tour jackets, t-shirts, sweatshirts and festival shirts.

For obvious reasons, usually, the lighting truss goes up first, leaving a clear stage for the backline, stage gear and the PA towers, which will be built on either side. The backline is the band's amplification system so named because it marks the back line of the artist's space on the stage. It will consist of guitar (both bass and lead) amplifiers, amplification and controls for the various keyboard set-ups. The cables are laid out before carpets or floor covering is put in place. Next come drum and keyboard risers, then the keyboards, amps, drum kits and finally the microphones. One or two times during the building of the infrastructure, they'll retire to the catering room where the tour caterers will have prepared something nourishing and healthy. Gone are the days of burgers, pizzas, fish & chips and when the, always slim, vegetarians would have been offered nothing more exotic than an omelette or cheese and bread.

By four o'clock, the majority of the crew's work is done and they'll start to prepare for the arrival of the artist for the sound check. This can be a brief five-minute affair or maybe up to two hours in the other extreme. Basically, it's to give the artist and (more importantly in this instance) their technicians a chance to check all of the equipment and set the sound levels for the particular venue they are playing in. Yes, the sound will change quite a bit when the audience takes their seats, but experienced sound engineers will take this factor into consideration.

The microphone is probably the single most important piece of equipment you'll get to use in your career. It's your gateway to the world, or at the very least, the audience in the Half Moon in Putney. In some instances the microphone is also a cool photo opportunity, as with say David Bowie, Dave Berry and Liam Gallagher. With others it's a much-needed prop, something to distract themselves with while they are performing – Roger Daltrey, Rod Stewart and Freddy Mercury being the pioneers in this group. But generally your microphone should be your vital link between your art and your audience. In the studio, you microphone is connected via a maze of toys and gadgets to the recording equipment, and while Playing Live it will be connected to your PA system.

It's probably worth noting here why a PA system (Public Address system) is needed in the first place and how it works.

Okay, you are in an empty ballroom, standing at the back. The singer starts to sing and you can just about hear him. Now add your drummer to keep the beat and the rhythm of the song. Once the drummer starts you, and the audience, are going to struggle to hear your singer. Next add in the bass guitar to lock the song solidly into the beat and add a bit more to the foundation. At the back of the ballroom you'll find the singer disappears even further into the sound. Next add in the rhythm guitar and/or an organ, which cements the top melody lines of the lead guitar, brass section and harmony vocals. Now, not only has your lead vocalist disappeared, but you'll probably find that the drums and bass will be drowning out your rhythm guitar, bits of your brass and most of your harmony vocals. Okay? Hold that thought and then imagine that the ballroom is filled with 2,000 people chatting and shuffling around in their seats. You'll probably only be able to hear the drums and feel the unpleasant thud of the bass in your chest.

So, the basic problem we have to overcome is to organise things so that each and every member of the audience can hear the band without having their heads blasted off. This balance of sound, and the band's ability to achieve it, is of paramount importance to a successful performance. So a PA system was developed and refined over the years.

We start with a microphone. The singer sings into the microphone. The microphone is a sensitive membrane and the singer's voice is translated, via pluses on the membrane, into an electronic signal. This signal in pluses and minuses is then transferred back into an amplifier, which enlarges this voice-generated-electronic-signal, using valves. The amplifier, in turn, passes this new amplified signal, via leads, into a speaker cabinet. The speaker cabinet is very similar to the reverse process of the microphone. The speakers in the cabinet translate these signals back into a louder reproduced version of the human voice and transmits this new electronically reproduced voice into the audience via the speaker cones. Additionally, in the middle of this elaborate process, you can divert your electronic signal through various distorting gadgets, such as echo units or other enhancing units to falsify the results. Knowing how the microphone works is one thing, but you also need to learn how to work the microphone. Some artists behave as though the microphone doesn't exist, but generally speaking all great artists seem to have a basic understanding of how to work the famous silver bullet and get the best out of it. Talk at length with your sound engineer about it. Never forget that no matter how cool you're looking up there on stage, no matter how hip the shapes you are throwing, if you're not singing properly "on mic" and giving a strong positive signal into your microphone, you've immediately compromised your sound engineer in his ability to bring the full qualities of your voice, and by extension your performance, to your audience.

I've seen too many name artists singing "off mic" to know that this is an issue they have never properly addressed in their performance career. You'll know you're getting it right when the end product of your voice sounds 100% natural. You want the audience to feel they are hearing you as though you were standing right beside them, singing into their ears, without the aid of microphones, amplifiers or speakers being involved in the process.

Then, of course, you do have the other extreme where, through the use of electronic technology in the form of a gadget called a "Voice

Tuner", your sound engineer can help you hit all the right notes should that be your particular weakness. Just think of the trick used with Cher's voice on her hit single 'I Believe'. You know that point in the song where the tone of her voice changes to sound slightly inhuman or machine-like? Well, the same piece of equipment can take duff notes and turn them into perfectly pitched ones. Just for the record, by the way, the single 'Bang Bang' shows Cher has a great natural voice. I imagine she has done her fair share of sound checks in her day.

At the end of the sound check, band and crew will sit down to dinner together. Sometimes the unfortunate principal of the band will have this moment stolen to catch up with promotional activities, either in a quiet room or on the old dog and bone.

Either way, the buzz backstage will have started. Artists are always desperate to get up on stage, no matter how bad their day has been, no matter how much they hate life on the road, that impending show time will be sure to start their hearts beating faster.

And what will the promoter be doing when all of this has been going on? Well, he'll swan in at the crack of dinner time to sample the delights of the act's catering.

He, or his rep, should be checking the security, the box office, checking in with the fire officer, discussing all aspects of safety, and checking that the stage has been dressed following the sound check/ rehearsal. There's nothing as ugly as an undressed stage with a CJ (Clapham Junction) of leads, or uncovered risers and opened flight and instrument cases lying about creating a mess.

The truth is that the promoter is now rarely more than a figurehead. There are teams of people doing everything. In the good old days, the promoter would do the divvy up at the end of the night directly with the manager. Nowadays, the promoter's accountant will do a 90-minute settlement (usually during the course of the artist's performance) with the artist's tour accountant. The promoter will still make sure he does a bit of back-slapping PR with the act, the manager or the agent to ensure he protects his position for the future. But with the arrival of the Clear Channel style of promoting, things have started to get very clinical. It is becoming more of an industry where the music comes way down on a long list of priorities.

I believe Clear Channel have assumed their position simply because agents and managers became lazy. Let me explain. Agents will generally take the easy way out. Instead of ringing Roger Eagle (God bless his soul for he certainly had one) for the Liverpool concert, John Tully for

Birmingham, Stuart Basford for Sheffield, Mark Mackie for Glasgow, Phil Jones for Manchester, Peter Bryson for Magherafelt, Gerald Palmer for Peterborough and John McIvor for Letterkenny, they were happier simply to ring one of the major London promoters who would take their act all around the country for say 25 shows, saving the agent the work of setting up 25 individual shows with 25 individual promoters. Going the national promoter route, the agent would probably make the same commission, maybe even a bit more, because nationwide promoters are always greedier. They tend to have a bit more clout with the record companies so they can usually get them to pay for some of their advertising or pay for the printing of the tour poster. Of course the quid pro quo is that the artist in question's latest release will be plastered all over the same posters and adverts. In my experience, however, local promoters are usually more fans of the music itself. They most certainly have a better local network of contacts. Again, in this instance – I'm talking about artists you *have* to promote, as opposed to artists where all the promoter has to do is make their tickets available – the best way to break a city is to work the city with someone who knows it, rather than someone doing it by numbers from London.

Fast forward the above system several years and you now have a situation where the agents are pissed off when managers take a leaf out of the agent's lazy book, and make one call to Clear Channel for their act's worldwide tour. There are two main advantages to the manager. He'll cream in lots more money and there'll be no agent's commission to boot.

From the outside, though, it appears that Clear Channel will burn itself out, so, in the long term, the future looks okay for the small promoter. This means that our Goggles Anonymous promoter can safely enjoy dinner with the band and fill the time by telling a few of his tales, you know, like how promoters have to deal with artists' egos and all the wheeling and dealing that goes on behind the scenes.

Stories about the time when Tanita Tikaram was just getting started and we put her on anywhere and everywhere, just to get her in front of an audience. She had a beautiful bunch of songs and was very happily going about picking up her stagecraft by supporting quality artists around town.

One week she opened for Warren Zevon at Hammersmith Odeon and the next she was due to open for John Martyn at the Sadler's Wells Theatre in Islington. Between confirming Tanita on the Sadler's Wells' bill and the show taking place, the promoter was persuaded to add

Tracy Chapman to the bill as well. This meant that Tanita was promoted from the opening act to the middle act.

Come concert day, all the artists duly performed their sound checks in the late afternoon. Tracy and her people were none to fussed about opening for an unknown from Basingstoke, so they retired to their hotel to freshen up before show time. They arrived back at the venue 40 minutes after they were due to appear, huffing and puffing about how impossible the London traffic was. They fully expected Miss Tikaram to have taken Miss Chapman's spot.

Not so.

"Oh, you're fine," the promoter said, greeting them at the stage door, "I knew the traffic would be bad, so I accounted for it in the stage times I gave you. You've on stage in five minutes."

That particular promoter was not thinking, "I better look after Tracy (or Tanita) because they are going to be big" – he was doing what was the right thing to do.

But that's just one of the easier episodes that promoters have to deal with. Sometimes their footwork is more akin to Fred Astaire than it is to the heavy metal merchants they have to deal with.

Catering has come a long way since the time one of Judas Priest's earlier promoters, who was also at that time their manager, mystified the band by providing a certain type of sandwich in the dressing room every night on a tour. The band grew suspicious, especially when the corners of the said sandwiches started to resemble Billy Fury's winklepickers. So, when their promoter's back was turned, they marked the sandwiches and noted to their amusement and distaste that exactly the same sandwiches turned up at the next several shows.

Nowadays on the road, catering is like a cookery master class. Catering companies such as Eat To The Beat will arrive with the crew at the crack of dawn, unpack their equipment and ovens from flight cases and start the day by preparing the crew's breakfast. There'll be snacks and nibbles available through to lunchtime when they'll be served a three-course meal. Then there'll be more dips and munchies until after the sound check when they'll be joined by the band members, promoters, record company personnel, friends or other road crews who happen to be in the same town that day but have a day off, boyfriends, girlfriends, husbands, and wives for a three-course evening meal. Then there'll be tea, coffee and sandwiches (unmarked) until the end of the load-out in the early hours of the morning.

All this means, of course, is that artists and crew have a chance to eat hot, healthy, nutritious food each and every day while they're on tour. It also means that musicians and crew can return home at the end of a tour with, in theory, their traditional per diems unspent and intact.

Naturally enough there will be wine and beer available in the catering room, but the majority of that part of the rider will appear in the artists' private dressing rooms and hospitality rooms where they'll conduct the after-show meet and greets.

Meal over, the band members will retire to the sanctuary of their dressing rooms, some to sleep off the large meal and others to prepare themselves for the evening concert.

14

THE CONCERT

Meanwhile, front of house, the doors are opened and eventually, following visits to the bar and the merchandising stall, the audience are encouraged to take their seats. The lights go down, the PA quietens and the band walks on stage in darkness under a growing cloud of dry ice. Applause starts as people pick out the star, or their favourite members of the band. Sometimes this can be difficult, especially with reluctant stars.

And there are few more reluctant than J.J.Cale. He's a very private man and is not into the star thing at all. In fact, I think he released quite a few albums before he was persuaded to put his photo on the sleeve, and it was the back of the sleeve at that. The first time we brought him over to the UK, I'm sure absolutely no one knew what he actually looked like.

Support act over, the roadies took the stage as they do, and started to dismantle the support artist's equipment and set up the main act's equipment. The venue in question was the Victoria Palace and there was an overwhelming air of excitement and anticipation. The roadies were busy working away and I could tell that a few members of the audience close to me – I always love to sit in the audience to personally experience our shows – were getting a bit restless and a bit annoyed by this bearded older roadie who was messing around with a clapped-out guitar, trying to get it to do something it obviously didn't want to do. I hate that, don't you? You're in the mood for a great concert. There's a magic atmosphere. I suppose it's a bit like being with a group of children waiting around together for a treat they know is coming. The prospect of the treat is ensuring they all behave well and there's a real feel-good vibe. Tingling is a word used often to describe it perfectly. But then, at the Victoria Palace, the mood was in danger of being ruined by this roadie chap who just won't give up on showing the

157

audience that he was also quite good on guitar; so good in fact that maybe he shouldn't be a roadie.

Then the lights go down and isn't the bearded roadie still on stage, with his back to the audience, working away on the guitar and on the amp, allowing the odd squeal and echo burp to escape. "He'd better hurry up and get the f**k off," I hear the girl next to me say to her companion. Most of the band is in place now, but this roadie chap *still* hasn't taken the guitar to the edge of the stage and passed it over to Mr. Cale.

"Heaven's above," the girl complains more loudly as the band strikes up into the first song with the roadie chap still on stage, and now, not only is he on stage, but he's actually being so insolent, he's also playing along with the band. Then he turns around reluctantly on stage and steps up to the microphone, and the girl beside me gasps in genuine shock as she recognises the unmistakable dulcet tones of Mr. J.J. Cale.

And the entire audience went ape.

*

I love to watch the way an artist takes the stage and starts his set. You can tell a lot about an artist in the first few minutes of the first song. You can tell how much the performance means to the artist. You can tell how much of an *act* they're putting on, how much they like being on stage and how much they like being on the road. You can tell a great deal about the interplay between the various band members and you can tell how aware the artist is of their audience.

The minute the first song finishes I love to look around at the audience and see how they are reacting to the artist. You can tell a lot by this reaction. Some artists, notably Bruce Springsteen, like to go crash bang wallop for three songs before they come up for air. Others like to come out and greet their audience and have a wee chat the way you'd do with a friend. The main thing to be aware of is that there is no single right way to do this. There is no scripted way for our band Goggles Anonymous to do their show. Their best chance of success is to do the show the way they feel it. And if they don't feel it, they'll never be able to bluff it enough to fool an audience.

As we'll discuss later, audiences don't know how to lie. Each member of the audience is just (obviously) a smaller part of the whole. Sometimes they are very supportive, however, sadly, at times, they can be extremely unforgiving. But equally they add to the energy, which is beyond even their control. This energy is very powerful and certainly very potent.

Christy Moore is an artist who has few equals when it comes to a solo performance. When he's up there, in full flow, you can tell how much he loves it, how much the performance takes him over. A few years ago, his playing live career was in jeopardy because he was suffering from a medical condition, which was severely aggravated on stage. It might have been that the rush of adrenalin an artist receives as a result of the energy of the audience was doing him harm or something, but either way it was proving very detrimental to his health and several times he ended up in hospital.

Christy thought about the problem a lot. He didn't want to give up performing – anyone who is that great must enjoy it immensely – so he started to analyse the situation. He worked out that the biggest charge he received from the audience was possibly when he walked out on stage. His audiences were so genuinely happy at the chance to see and hear him perform live that they just couldn't hide their feelings. Multiply this by the number of people in the audience and it's probably something similar to enjoying a couple of thousand sexual experiences simultaneously!

His solution, when he started gigging again after his illness, was to do the sound check, but then, instead of leaving the stage the way all artists do – to allow the audience to enter the venue – he remained sitting on the stage. His logic was that if he sat up there chatting away with his two friends, musicians and fellow travellers, Donal Lunny and Declan Sinnott, then he would experience the audience in twos, threes and fours as they casually drifted into the venue and this way he'd avoid the charge he felt as he walked out on stage when they were all seated, waiting for him, the anticipation dripping from the walls of the venue like sweat. Christy is still fine-tuning his new methods of playing live, but the good news is that it's working, he's in fine health and enjoying it again without a dark cloud hanging over him.

Something else that never ceases to amaze me is the direction a concert might take. Each one seems to have a life of its own. Here, let me explain. Okay, let's say Goggles Anonymous is playing an important gig and it's sold out. They write out their set list before-hand. The support act goes down as well as any support act can, the audience retires to the bar, the merchandising stall or remain in their seats chatting to their mates trying to guess the set list or star-spot. Which reminds me, years ago we had Loudon Wainwright III (another very powerful solo performer) playing a sell-out concert in the National Stadium in Dublin. Now the Irish media, God bless them, always had a habit of looking over your shoulder when you were trying to check them off the pest list – sorry of course I meant guest list – to see who else might be attending the concert. So, on this particular night, I included the names John Lennon and Dylan on the guest list and made sure I gave the media present ample time to clock the names as I checked the list for theirs. Sure enough, the following day, there were a couple of pieces in the papers saying: "Dylan and Lennon in town to see Loudon Wainwright."

Back to Goggles Anonymous though. The band will be going through their pre-gig ritual in the interval. Singers can usually be heard in some distant corner of the backstage area loosening up their vocal cords by doing their scales – Elvis Costello sounds like he's at the Kop (vocally) supporting his favourite team when he does his. The wardrobe mistress, or one of the roadies, depending on the status of the act, will have everything nicely ironed up for the occasion. Robert Plant irons his white t-shirt prior to going on. Honest to goodness, I kid you not. Asgard programmes the Acoustic Stage at Glastonbury and Mr. Plant has been kind enough to appear on two memorable occasions. The second time he nipped into our production office 20 minutes before show time and proceeded to iron his t-shirt, chatting away as he went about the task. He always likes to wear a crisp white t-shirt, which is fine in itself. It was just such a surprise to see one of the world's biggest stars doing it himself. Ah well, I suppose we should expect no less for such a fan of music as Robert. Phil May of The Pretty Things wore a brand new set of white Levi jeans for every performance, or maybe it was every day of his life.

Anyway, pre-gig ritual over, the lights go down and the band takes the stage to start their set. Now when a band is new and you're their agent, you generally sit in the audience willing them through their performance, hoping they're playing the right song at the right time. When they don't, and they lose the audience's attention, you'll will them with all your might to do such and such a song, because you know it will put them back on track again. Perhaps they feel they need to keep that particular song for later in the set as a safety device to win an encore. At the same time you are thinking, "If you don't pick it up again quickly, you'll lose the audience altogether." It's like when you, as the artist's representative, go to record company meetings where singles will be discussed and invariably the conversation will turn to everyone's favourite song on the album, the definitive single. Then the clever clogs at the record company will suggest, "No, let's keep the best single 'til later. Let's put out the second or third best single now and then, as phase two," you know to get from Platinum (300,000) to double Platinum, "let's go with the best song." Wrong! Big mistake. You might never get to your second single if the first one flops, so you bury your album. If you've got a sure-fire hit, don't let them try and be clever on your behalf – get it out immediately. Have your hit, then start to consider phase two. Equally, if the record company says to you, "There are lots of favourites on this album," be aware that's code for, "There are no real hits on this album."

You're on stage, though, and the last thing on your mind will be hit singles. Well, certainly the last thing on your mind *should* be hit singles. Having said that about your stagecraft, building a good set is important, I wonder if it really does matter. If the magic is there and the audience is tuned in and they're with you, for whatever reason, all of this is outside of your control, even outside the audience's control. Do you know what I mean? Take Van Morrison at The Rainbow for instance. That series of concerts was the basis of one of the best live albums ever released. You can actually hear the natural organic excitement of the audience on the record, and I'm quite sure Van Morrison, no matter what he chose to include, couldn't have changed that, even if he'd wanted to.

The thing about Van though is that every single person who used to work with him has his or her VM stories, which are swapped around and have, no doubt, become embellished over the years. For example, Van was rehearsing a new band and had a new crew for a tour, and at the appointed hour all except Van were present in the rehearsal room. This geezer walks in, long coat, dark hat and every inch, "a working man in his prime". The sound engineer takes one look at him and calls out to the rest of his colleagues: "Anyone order a taxi?"

The stranger in the long coat walks up and mumbles to the sound engineer in his broad Americanised Ulster accent, "No, I'm Van."

The sound engineer completely mis-hears him and shouts out again, "Sorry, did anyone order a van?"

*

When you're hot, you'll attract the liggers. Liggers are party-orientated people who love to be at places they feel it's cool to be. The rarer the party, backstage lig, happening or whatever, the more the liggers *have* to be there. Liggers are not primarily interested in the music. All they really desire is to get backstage. And you know what? There are few places I've come across that are as boring as backstage at concerts. Generally this hallowed space consists of small, horrible, badly painted dressing rooms. Musicians would be forgiven for thinking that when the majority of venues were being built, the backstage area was either added on as an afterthought when the budget was completely spent, or had been forgotten about altogether.

The most potent currency for liggers is the Backstage Pass. Those with the **A**ccess **A**ll **A**reas, Laminate Pass – or "the illuminate Pass" as Ted Hawkins used to call them – may go as they please any night of the tour. Then you have a series of coloured "stickies" for local crew members, local promoter, the record company staff, family (not wives, girlfriends or boyfriends though, they possess the magic Laminate – complete with multicoloured lanyard – that's the bit of string hung around your neck to which the valuable Laminate is attached).

The more successful the show the more the need there is to lig. Conversely, when a show is dying, liggers will be as thin on the ground as silent roadies. If the show's not selling at all, then you literally can't give your tickets and guest passes away. But the great thing about liggers is that they give hours of amusement to you and your family members, thereby filling those awkward tongue-tied minutes when they come back and see you after the show. For further information on this subject see the movie *In Bed With Madonna* with Kevin Costner looking like he's been press-ganged into coming back to say hello for the cameras. Kevin, with his careful choice of the word "neat", proved to be the better mannered of the two.

Backstage stories can be enlightening as well. Van Morrison was out with a mate of mine and they were both going to a Bob Dylan concert that particular evening at Wembley. My mate stops off at Van's place so Van can freshen up and change his jacket and they duly head off to Wembley. After the concert, Dylan, John McEnroe, Van and George Harrison are backstage and they're all chatting away. Van searches his jacket for something and starts to panic. He starts to complain that someone has stolen his wallet.

George chips in, "I may be from Liverpool Van, but I didn't steal your wallet."

Hearty laughs all around and all's well that ends well. When Van changed his jacket on his way to Wembley he forgot to move his wallet from one jacket to the other.

*

Concert over, the artists, such as Goggles Anonymous, will go home, warm with the memories of stories such as the above and you'll relive your finest moments. You'll recall how well the band played, how fresh the material sounded and how amazingly well the audience reacted to the show. As a badge of honour, you'll carry into your dreams your three encores, proof as to how well you played and how much the audience enjoyed your performance.

The following morning, you'll buy the papers, read the reviews and not only will you think the reviewer is talking about a different concert, but you'll convince yourself that you're not worthy of appearing on stage again.

The one big baddie, though, the "he's behind you!" character, is the reviewer.

The thing you have to remember is that reviewers mostly want to work in fiction, so it's important you, the public and artists, ignore their words whether they be good or bad. It's important to note though, that reviewers gain more attention if they speak ill of you. Enough said.

15

THE FESTIVALS

Regardless of my personal taste, festivals have become *the* thing over the last decade.

Rock'n'roll is now big and sophisticated enough to be able to put on a show which will attract and satisfy 100,000 plus people. Festivals are a completely different animal and you literally have to play to the back hedge to have any chance of succeeding.

The old LCD (lowest common denominator) theory will stand you in good stead and a bit of Chuck Berry, Beatles or a string of your hits is a must. We've been involved in Glastonbury one way or another over the years and it's still the festival against which all other festivals are measured. Michael Eavis is not a professional promoter in that he does not make his living from promoting concerts or festivals, yet he is the only festival organiser to realise that the vital ingredients for a festival are *variety* and *fun*. An important thing to realise is that a large percentage of the Glastonbury audience never goes near a music stage over the entire weekend. Many go simply for the weekend's craic. (In this instance, I'm using the Irish definition of the word, craic, that is – fun and frivolity – and not the English – chemical substance – version.) They go to meet friends and hang out and know that whatever takes their fancy when it comes to the arts of New Age will be there, literally, with bells on.

The problem with festivals, from the point of view of the live circuit, is that if you're not careful you can condense a couple of month's worth of appearances up and down the country into one 50 minute spot on the main stage.

Equally, for a mid-range artist a successful key appearance at Glastonbury can propel you quite a few feet up that slippery slope in one single afternoon. On the other hand, if you die a death on the major outdoor stage, you could very well not just end up back at square one but you could find yourself having to throw a couple of sixes – and maybe even a lead guitarist – before you are allowed to move again.

My favourite Michael Eavis quote? Asked if he found it difficult, as a farmer, to negotiate with all these rock'n'roll stars, he replied, "Not at all," without blinking an eyelid. "Sure it's just like buying cattle!"

For all of his innocence, he's nobody's fool and he does tend to hide behind the, "Oh sure, I'm only a farmer" line, so much so that most of the agents don't see him coming until he's gone. On top of which, he knows his bands, old and new, like few others do.

Knowing Michael, I'm sure he'd never have got himself in the situation that the Castle Donington Festival promoter did a few years ago, when he booked Kiss and Ozzy Osbourne as the co-headliners.

Co-headlining or equal top billing is a myth. It doesn't exist. At the end of the day, there is only one name that can go on the top of the advert or the poster, or one name that goes to the right-hand side if both artists are on the same line. Promoters have various ways of getting around it. One artist gets to be top on the posters, the other on the adverts. But even then, there is only one act that can play the genuine top of the bill.

Let's hear it for Ozzy!

Anyway it was all set up and Ozzy's tour manager arrived on the site first, mindful that the early bird gets the worm. He checked out his dressing room (portacabin) and then just to make sure everything *was* equal he stole a look at Kiss' accommodation. He discovered by the use of a slide rule, measuring tape and various set squares, that a mortal sin had been committed.

Hadn't the promoter only given Kiss one extra sofa in their accommodation?

Now, I need you to imagine you're on the set of *Spinal Tap* to be able to visualise all the shapes being thrown. Where's reality television when you really need it? The promoter and his people checked high and low in furniture stores, antique stores, hotel lobbies, discount stores, local production manager's granny's house, all to no avail. They couldn't find that important extra matching sofa.

Solution to the problem? Simple. You can make things equal not only by adding but also by subtracting.

So they simply removed one sofa from Kiss' dressing room. Ozzy had his equality and the Castle Donington's promoter's production office was the most luxurious it had ever been.

Dressing room accommodation for artists at festivals is a bit like movie stars location mobile homes. In fact it's a *lot* like it, the bigger and the snazzier the accommodation, the bigger the status of the star. Or maybe it's a variation on that. There are actually companies who will provide the service for you of putting the *dressing* in dressing room. The secret is to make the artists feel at home. I mean the real secret is not to make them feel too much at home, you don't want the artists retiring with cocoa, a pipe and slippers just as they're meant to be taking the stage, but I think you know what I mean.

One resourceful festival promoter came up with a very novel and inexpensive way of furnishing the artists' dressing rooms. A few weeks before his festival, while driving around town, he noticed that Asda were offering this amazing deal. They were guaranteeing a full money back refund within one month if the customer was not fully satisfied with the product.

Now there was an offer too difficult to resist.

*

You remember I told you about the Tanita Tikaram and Tracy Chapman incident at Sadler's Wells? Well, a couple of years and a couple of million albums sales each later, they shared a bill again. This time it was in Norway and at an outdoor festival. Tanita was number one in Norway for 16 weeks with her first album *Ancient Heart*. It sold so many copies there, apparently, even the reindeers were seen making purchases.

Just outside of Oslo is this very picturesque island called the Isle of Calf and each summer they hold an outdoor concert, which attracted an average of 12,000 people. In the previous three years I'd booked Van Morrison, Jackson Browne and Santana as the main acts and as Tanita had already played everywhere else there was to play in Norway, I thought this would be a great event for her. Luckily enough the promoter agreed and we did a deal. Then someone had the great idea of adding Tracy Chapman to the bill. As she was going to have to get on to the island early in the morning before the crowds there was no fear of a repeat performance of the Sadler's Wells incident.

They asked for top billing.

"Sorry, Tanita's already top of the bill."

"Okay, in that case we'd like equal top," they said.

The promoters asked me what I felt about this. I repeated my oft-used phrase, "There is only one top of the bill. Whoever is listed top or on the right and whoever goes on last is top of the bill."

In this instance that wasn't strictly the case; the main act always went on second to last with the play-out act going on last to ensure there wasn't a massive surge for the limited bridge access to the mainland.

So, as long as Tanita was top left on the adverts and posters, played the main slot, received her handsome fee I wasn't really concerned. The deal was finalised and went on sale.

It sold well.

And then it sold some more.

And then the cent dropped in the other camp that they didn't really have equal top billing because *equal top billing doesn't really exist.* So they were on to the promoter and the promoter, who was stuck between a rock and a hard place, due to the healthy ticket sales, was on to me. I could hear down the telephone line the ping, ping, pinging of him pulling his hair out.

I just happened to have a copy of his poster in my office as I spoke to him.

"These posters of yours," I offered, hoping to be helpful. "I mean, I'm not meaning to be rude or anything, but erm, they're . . . well . . . they're not very expensive looking."

"Ah, but this is Norway, Paul, they're the best posters you can get here."

"I know, I know, but erm, they're not very *expensive* looking, are they?" I repeated, hoping my italics were travelling across the North Sea.

"But they're the only posters we can get printed here."

"Yes . . . uhm, but they didn't cost you a lot of money, did they?" I persisted.

"No," he admitted.

"So, if say you wanted to run up another 10 or so posters with, let's say for argument's sake, a slight variation on the artwork, I mean, it wouldn't be an expensive exercise, would it?"

"No?"

"And then, if you felt you needed to send those particular posters to say someone else who might also be on the bill, and you know giving you a bit of a hard time . . ."

The krone dropped loudly and the gig was saved.

And finally on festivals . . . there was the famous instance at an Italian festival when Uriah Heep wouldn't go on stage because they believed the stage was unsafe. An armed guard took out his machine gun and fired a few rounds into the tyres of the band's buses and trucks! Suddenly the stage became a very safe place to escape to.

16

THE AUDIENCE

The applause of a responsive audience is *the* ultimate music to an artist's ear. I have found that there are two things to which artists react very positively. One is the recognition applause that comes a few bars into the start of their more popular songs and the second is when an audience starts to sing along with the song. Surely there can be fewer bigger compliments an audience can pay an artist. It's quite magical when you hear an audience with a voice of one – usually joyous, sometimes, because of the predominant baritone blend, a little solemn – join in and even – as is often the case in Belfast – take over a song. For me the other magical thing is when a band, or an artist, start straight into the next song before the applause to the previous one has died down; by doing so, they manage to carry the audience's energy straight to the next tune. Something like the intro to Paul Simon's 'You Can Call Me Al' works wonderfully under such conditions.

The recognition applause seems to happen in two waves. The first one when the musicians start into the music and the anorak, train spotter or ardent fan starts up the applause. The second wave follows, usually a matter of bars later, when the average fans recognise the first lines of the lyrics they remember so well. They will either start to clap with all their might or shoot half a roll of film capturing you singing your famous lyric. There is in fact a live Paul Simon album that demonstrates these two levels of recognition perfectly if not somewhat ludicrously.

When the audience are not, shall we say, the most receptive or supportive, say in somewhere like Baden-Baden, artists have been heard to address the auditorium with, "Excuse me, but have any of you ever been an audience before?"

I've been doing this one way or another now for 30 plus years and I still don't fully understand the genesis of an audience – your audience; any audience. You put your tickets on sale – it might be for a pub, which holds a hundred or so people, or it might be for Michael Jackson's record-breaking seven-night run at Wembley Stadium a few years back – and a certain amount of people buy tickets and turn up for the event. The same applies to sports, the cinema, and the theatre. People just turn up. Why do they turn up? Why, sometimes, do they decide not to turn up?

The closest comparison I can come up with is the process you go through when you are lighting a fire. You can have your fireplace packed perfectly with newspaper twists, twigs, small sticks, larger sticks, logs, coal and more logs. If you set it all up properly, all you have to do is light the corner of one of the paper twists with a match and whoosh! Your fire has taken and your hearth is filled with cheek-flushing flames. My dad's an expert at it. All he needs is a little paper, a few bits of wood and coal and he can get it going immediately every single time. I, on the other hand, can have all of the above and even cheat a bit with fire lighters, not to mention (sometimes) an entire box of matches, but it doesn't matter how much I huff and puff, I still won't be able to create a fire.

So you see why I sometimes think that the creation of an audience is somewhat similar. You can have all of your set-up perfectly in place with posters, adverts, leaflets, newspaper stories, radio plugs, television plugs, a mention on the artist's website. Then you try to ignite the fire by putting the tickets on sale and . . . no whoosh! The obvious difference between making a fire and making an audience is that there is a secret to lighting a fire. My father knows this secret. In the music business though, no one has the secret of creating the audience.

It's like, the morning after the Brighton concert this agent who is out on tour with one of his main acts goes out for a walk on the beach and he comes across this genie bottle, or at least it looks like what he imagines a genie bottle would look like. So just for the craic, he rubs the bottle and guess who appears? Great, you're on the case; a genie appears. First off, the agent tries to sign the genie to an exclusive contract. The genie refuses, apparently he's developing his own pantomime and game show, so he wants to keep his options open. He does however tell the agent that he will grant him one wish. The agent asks what's happened to the traditional three wishes. The genie reminds the agent that they are in the middle of a recession and cutbacks are necessary.

The agent sits down on a bench close to the pier and unconsciously counts the number of people going on to the pier as he tells the genie that he suffers from a fear of flying. He knows it's stupid but he just can't get into an aeroplane. On top of which, he's equally scared of boats and ships but he'd really love to go to America. Since he was a kid he's been in love with the Lone Ranger & Tonto, baseball & basketball, diners that serve hash browns, eggs over easy, pancakes with maple syrup and that's just breakfast, all-day movies, book stores that last for blocks, music being played on every street corner, Elvis Presley, Bob Dylan, The Beach Boys, Superman Comics, sunshine, beautiful girls, "have a nice day" and "y'all come back now, ya hear."

"Okay, Okay," the Genie sighs, "I get the picture. So what's your wish?"

"Well, I thought if you could build me a motorway across the sea I could nip over there when I wanted. I'd also be able to pick up representation of a few great artists," the agent replies.

"Get real," the Genie screeches in a fit of laughter, "that's nearly impossible; try another wish?"

"Okay," the agent replies. "Teach me how to understand the audience?"

The Genie stops hovering around and swooshes down to sit on the bench beside the agent. "Okay, now about this transatlantic motorway of yours, just how many lanes did you say you wanted?"

I've hung around many a venue entrance hall, marvelling at people as they turn up in twos and threes and sometimes even solo. That is if they turn up at all. There is always that horrible feeling of emptiness in the pit of your stomach at the prospect that no one might show up at all to see your artist. But then they start to arrive in dribs and drabs, and the relief you feel is akin to getting the all-clear from your dentist while lying petrified in their chair. I know of no greater relief. The doors open at say seven o'clock and the artist is meant to go on at eight. The audience will trickle in, the last one miraculously taking his seat just as the house lights dim.

I am still so in awe of this body of people showing up. Sometimes you have an opportunity to use this time effectively by giving out flyers for your other forthcoming shows, a practice known as leafleting. You can learn so much from an audience during this time. I remember once I was handing out leaflets at a BB King concert in Hammersmith Odeon. The concert wasn't one of ours, but it was the perfect target audience for a forthcoming concert we were promoting in the same venue with The Robert Cray Band. We were taking a major step up with Robert. His previous concert had been in the Electric Ballroom in

Camden Town. The Electric Ballroom is about half the capacity of Hammersmith Odeon but we felt it would work. The Robert Cray Band was on the rise and there was a bit of a buzz around him and his band. He has a sweet, soulful voice, he plays guitar like a veteran and, on top of all that, he had natural talent and he looked really cool. He was just maybe a wee bit too young and good-looking to take up his position amongst the blues greats at that point. Anyway, we'd spent quite a bit of money on advertising the concert. We'd taken our adverts in the usual papers: *The Sunday Times, The Evening Standard, Time Out* and *NME.* We'd printed and distributed our posters. Now, although the tickets were selling okay, they weren't exactly flying out the door and I was shocked as I handed out the leaflets to find that people were hearing about the show for the first time. There was genuine surprise and interest emulating from the BB King punters. You see, sometimes you take your expensive adverts and print and distribute your beautiful posters and no one notices either, no one that is except the artist, the manager, the agent and the promoter. Real humans who buy their papers don't stop at every advert and take in all the details. Generally they pass by the adverts without a glance. But you stick a leaflet in the hand of a blues fan on his way into a venue to see BB King and there is a good chance he will want to buy a ticket for Robert Cray. And that is exactly what happened. The BB King audience went out over the next few weeks and bought their Robert Cray Band tickets and then, when you have a couple of thousand people walking around with Robert Cray Band Hammersmith Odeon tickets in their wallets, that is the *best* advert you can get, because they talk to their mates about it and pretty soon those 2,000 tickets become 2,500 tickets and then it's a short hop to 3,000 tickets and very soon you've sold out at 3,400 tickets. The house sold out and Robert Cray did the rest. It was a magic concert.

When the audiences don't appear, we, agents and promoters, have a long list of reasons to offer artists and managers.

1. It's school and college exam time.
2. It's school and college holiday time.
3. Mott The Hoople or Westlife were here last night.
4. The Quo or Coldplay are here tomorrow night.
5. There's been a non-stop run of concerts and the market place is saturated.
6. People were expecting a bus/tube/train strike.
7. There *was* a bus/tube/train strike.

8. The ticket price might have been just a wee bit too high.
9. The ticket price might have been just a wee bit too low.
10. The Promoter is just back from holiday.
11. The single was late appearing in the shops.
12. The single was too early, people have already forgotten it.
13. There is never an excuse number 13. It's too much like bad luck.
14. The album hasn't come out yet and people like to familiarise themselves with the new music before they come and see you live.
15. Music is no longer the priority it once was in young people's lives.
16. Either Inspector Morse or Inspector Christy Kennedy is on television tonight.
17. Kids spend all their time surfing the net these days.

And on and on you can go, and yes, some of these reasons will be valid reasons, but at the same time, Oasis can put two shows on sale for Knebworth (400,000 tickets give or take a hundred thousand) in the middle of exams or in the middle of a tube and train strike, they'll make *one* announcement and before they get a chance to advertise it properly, both shows will be sold out, with twice the number of requests for tickets as there are tickets available.

Why do we listen to music in the first place? For enjoyment, I suppose; for comfort, for companionship, to have a soundtrack for our thoughts, to have a special place we know we can return to each and every time we put on a particular piece of music.

How do audiences decide which music they like and which artist's concerts they are going to? The reality is subconsciously we probably start by enjoying the music our parents or our older siblings are listening to. Then, just as we turn 10 or 11, we start to show some form of independence and go off to explore our own tastes or tune in to what our schoolmates are listening to. Then we hear something we like with a passion. All of a sudden music is totally absorbing and the whole aspect of the live performance of it intrigues us. Before records, music was kept alive by live performances, but if the sales figures are anything to go by, live music is more popular than ever. So, we've left the original reason far behind and replaced it with a more social one; it's now as much a form of social interaction. Audiences separated by language, colour or religion come together as one to enjoy the music being made.

So, where does your audience, you the artist, yes that's Goggles Anonymous we are talking about, where does *your* audience come from? If, on your way to the top, you play Hammersmith Odeon (3,400 capacity) and sell it out, does this mean that someone else (Michael Bolton for instance) has lost 3,400 members of his audience? The truth is that you share your audience with several artists. Long gone are the days when you liked *only* The Beatles *or* The Rolling Stones. Assuming audiences are shared, how is your audience made up? It would be very easy if we were able to compartmentalise them, say if you liked The Beatles we could conclude you would also like A, B & C, but if you liked The Rolling Stones, then you'd like only X, Y & Z.

I love the music of Bob Dylan (for this example I picked someone I don't, unfortunately, work with). But I don't particularly like what Michael Bolton does. Sadly however, I am sure there *are* people who like Bob Dylan who also love Michael Bolton's work. I know, I know, but *you* tell *me* why? I've never been able to figure it out.

You see, when it comes to audiences, none of us really know who they are or where they come from. Why will they decide to go and see their favourite artist one night and thoroughly enjoy the evening, yet the next time the same artist is on tour they'll vote with their feet by staying away?

For my part, when I go to an amazing show like the ones I mentioned earlier – say Van Morrison at The Rainbow Theatre in London, Rockpile at Loughborough University, The Blue Nile at The Dominion Theatre in London, The Kinks at The Bilzen Festival, Jackson Browne at The Palladium in New York, or Genesis (with Peter Gabriel) at The Alexandra Theatre in Birmingham – I am so moved that I have trouble putting my feelings into words. At all of the above concerts – and here again I have picked concerts I wasn't involved with, although I have been lucky enough to subsequently work with five of these six artists – I could feel the hairs on the back of my neck stand up, I could feel my eyes well up, I couldn't have talked to anyone even if I'd wanted to.

I was *moved* by the power of the music.

I counted myself very lucky, not to say privileged, to have been present on those six occasions and to have witnessed what were, for me, the perfect shows. But I bet that on the six nights I am talking about, there were people in the audience who were not as captivated by the music as I was. You know, I'm sure there were people there only because their boyfriends, girlfriends, wives or husbands insisted they be there or persuaded them to be there. It's a bit like the great story Ned Sherrin tells about an empty seat at a hit show in theatreland.

The story goes that during an incredible run of a fabulously successful show – you know, sold out for years, tickets like gold dust – the theatre manager was doing his pre-curtain-up check of the audience. To his horror he discovered an empty seat. He checked with the box-office manager who confirmed that every seat in the house had been sold and paid for. When the theatre posts their "Full House" sign, they like the theatre to be truly full. So the manager went to the lady sitting next to the empty seat and asked if she knew to whom the seat belonged. She told the manager it was her husband's, he couldn't be there, but she was so looking forward to the amazing show she decided she just had to come by herself.

"But does he realise what he's missing?" the theatre manager enquired. "This is the hottest show in town. The touts are selling tickets on the streets for hundreds of pounds."

"I know," the woman replied, "I'm so looking forward to it. I bought our tickets five months ago and I can't wait for the show to start."

The manager thought that perhaps the woman and her husband had split up, so maybe he shouldn't pursue this line any further.

"But what about your friends," he said, still clearly in shock. "Didn't any of your friends want to come with you."

"No they couldn't," the woman replied. "They're all at my husband's funeral!"

So a hot ticket is always a hot ticket, but hot tickets can never be created by the business, it's made hot by the audience who buy the tickets.

The important point to remember in all of this is that there is one thing Goggles Anonymous and your promoter and your record company can never buy, and that's the buzz. When there is a buzz around on an artist, there is really little need for promotion, you just put the tickets or CDs on sale, and the buzz does the rest. The buzz is as effective as the magic touch my father uses when he's lighting his fire.

You, the artist, can make a great record, you can do all the things you're meant to do with it and your record just may, or may not, sell. But if there is a buzz on your record, just sit back and get ready to feel the heat.

The buzz usually happens at the beginning of your career and that's because newness is one of the vital ingredients for the buzz. Mind you, that's not necessarily always the case of course. Take for instance Paul Simon and *Graceland*. Really there was no apparent logical reason why that album happened the way it did. Mr. Simon was coming off the back of an album, *Hearts And Bones*, which hadn't done very well sales-wise. But even before *Graceland* was released, there was a buzz about it. The buzz happens when people start to talk about an artist or an artist's particular album. The buzz is effective because the people talking the album up are not just the people who are working on the album. The people I am referring to are agents, managers, promoters, radio produc-ers, television producers, journalists, DJs and general music fans who work within the music business community. All of these (and more) were buzzing about how special *Graceland* was, saying that it was a won-derful piece of work, which would do incredibly well and it did. It was the same thing with *Time Out Of Mind*, Dylan's last album.

This was Dylan's 44th album, so how are you meant to know if it would be a better or worse album than say, for instance, album number 29? And who even cares about that anyway? Bob Dylan released an album called, *Time Out Of Mind*. It was so good it caused a buzz, sold two million copies and won him three Grammies. Mind you, Dylan is in a different league altogether, isn't he? I think people will be discussing Dylan in a hundred years' time, the same way they discuss Dickens and Shakespeare today. You just see if I'm not right on that one.

At the time I am writing this, the Buzz is currently on Nora Jones, but by the time you read this, it will be on someone else and whoever it is will be as big as sliced bread. But you know the kind of artists I mean. They come from (apparently) nowhere and before you know it, they're a household name. Eva Cassidy is a great example. In her case it's obvi-ously very sad that she didn't receive any of that attention or all those sales until after her untimely death.

I suppose the point about discussing this audience thing is simply to warn you what may or may not happen to you and your career. There is a chance you could make an absolutely amazing album and all of your family, friends and business associates will agree with you about just how excellent it is, and then you'll release it and it may do nothing. Just like there's no guarantee that just because you form a group, you're going to get a record deal. Equally there's no guarantee that if you get a record deal, you are going to succeed. It seems to help a little if you can hang in there for a few years, I'm talking several years here, and provid-ing you've been professional all along the way, eventually you'll receive your 15 minutes of glory.

So, you know, just keep knocking on the door, refusing to go away. Keep making good music. Once the industry sees you around for a certain amount of time they eventually suss that you are not going to go away quietly. They start to think, "Oh well, if they're still playing to an audience after all this time, they must be doing something right, let's give them a break." They accept you as being part of the order of things and allow you to step up and take your place in the spotlight.

Equally, if you don't get that golden opportunity it's not anyone's fault, it just means that your music didn't strike a chord of sympathy with the audience that we are all so interested in.

The other thing you have to compete against is the current state of the British Recording Industry, *circa* 2003. It is certainly in bad shape but no worse than it's been before. Well okay, maybe it is! Last time around it was saved by the likes of Stiff Records, Chiswick Records, Berkeley Records and a few other fiercely independent labels who all gave it the much needed kick up the arse.

What did the big labels do with this skyward encouragement? Did they go out and find some singers of their own, or find themselves some great new groups? Did they heck. They liked the independents so much, they went out and bought them. They figured they didn't need to cultivate their relationships with new groups and artists and nurture them through the difficult early stages of their career. No, not at all. The "cheque book A&R" was a system they understood and preferred so they went off and bought themselves into the punk movement and success via the small labels. This time it's not going to be as easy. This time there are no independents or movements there to save them. The only movement the current record companies are going to experience is a laxative-induced one.

It's interesting to note that whereas Jake Riviera started Stiff Records with a £400 loan, Rob Dickens' Instant Karma Records drew a lot heavier on Sony Music's millions. Stiff, as we know, broke a few dozen great acts, yet when Sony and Instant Karma parted ways I don't think they'd chalked up their first success!

Good music always wins through though, and say you, the artist, do make your *Blonde On Blonde* or *Astral Weeks* or *I'm Alive* or *Hats* or *Abbey Road*, who's to say that you're going to be able to successfully repeat the process? And who's to say that it's guaranteed you're going to repeat it for a second, third or fourth album, or annually for several years like the record company will want to contract you to do?

I'm afraid it's not so easy to tap into something that special. It's not a coal seam you are mining. These little gems we are discussing just don't give themselves up that easily. No, it's much more difficult than that. A more likely road would be that you release your first album, the album that gains you the attention you are seeking. Then your next album just might be your breakthrough album, and should sell by the proverbial truckload. This album will be followed by a couple of albums that will benefit directly from your breakthrough album. Next you'll have several albums of diminishing return. Then this downward spiral in sales will be parachuted only by your often-resisted Greatest Hits album.

As I say, it's not easy to continuously produce hit singles or hit albums. And why? I don't really know. You see, I'm just part of that audience we've been discussing in this chapter. For my part, it might have something to do with the fact that when I have a copy of Leonard Cohen's *Songs From A Room*, I'm happy. I can listen to it whenever I want and maybe that's all I need from that particular artist. In the music business though, we want the audience to buy every single album an artist releases. We also want them to buy a ticket for every single time the artist tours. I suppose, considering the audiences other commitments and responsibilities, that's being just a wee bit unrealistic, isn't it?

The majority of artists I know and work with get it right though. They produce the best work that they can, work they are happy with and proud to put their name to, and the rest is down to that mythical undeterminable audience.

17

THE END BIT

If and when you achieve success, you'll be presented with a different set of problems to deal with.

Things like income tax. Obviously you'll have an expensive team of accountants to help you with this. Just in case you're tempted to hand the entire matter of your finances over to them, you'll be reminded of the high profile cases like Sting, Pink Floyd and Billy Joel who were similarly inclined and ended up paying for it more dearly than they'd intended. No matter how much money you are generating, you can never, ever afford to take your eye off that particular ball. If you do, it's sad to have to report that you'll deserve all you (don't) get.

For some reason, artists and money have proved to be strange bed-fellows. That applies to both making it and spending it. Just check out Michael Jackson's shopping spree on the controversial 2003 TV documentary for proof of this. "I don't know, but there it is," as Harry Worth used to say. Yep, a lot of artists seem to have a hard time getting to grips with the subtleties of money.

A mate of mine, a tour manager, was on the road once with San Francisco's Flaming Groovies. As he'd be driving them around Europe – they did particularly well in France and the Scandinavian territories – he'd hear them in the back of the van discussing how each of them was going to spend the $10,000 profit they individually reckoned they were going to take home from the tour.

Now this tour manager had done the costings for the tour and he knew for a fact they would be lucky to come out of the tour with a mere $1,000 each. Now this was years ago, when $1,000 still meant something, but obviously not as much as $10,000!

Eventually the tour manager felt that he couldn't travel around in their company any longer with them under the misapprehension that they were making a killing on the tour.

He advised them of what he knew to be the accurate figures.

The band members protested that they had indeed seen his expense figures for the tour, and the list of fees from the agent. They subtracted the expenses from the total fees and divided the balance by five. They assured the tour manager they'd checked and rechecked their figures and were quite convinced they were coming out with $10,000 each.

The tour manager persisted. It was not that he had a death wish, it was more that he knew full well that now the issue had been raised, if he allowed it to be brushed under the carpet the entire sorry mess would end up his fault. "But you mentioned this in Baden-Baden and we showed you how we arrived at the figures and you never said we were wrong. So, by a process of elimination and deduction, it's your fault."

The agent was summoned to attend the next gig, which, co-incidently, was handy for him as it was The Mean Fiddler in London. They wanted him to sort the matter out once and for all.

They gave him their costings, expenses versus income, and all at once he saw a crowd, a host of daft figures.

The expenses were, as ever with this tour manager, accurate to a penny. But the mistake, the big mistake was discovered on the income page. The problem proved to be a simple, yet costly one.

Although the agent had listed all of the fees in the local currency, the band had considered the fees to be in dollars. Now $20,000 is a lot of money, but 20,000 French Francs or 20,000 Norwegian Krone is worth less than 10% of the dollar figure.

So, the lesson to be learnt is that when you're looking at your fees, don't see what you want to see. Try and make sure you actually see (and understand) what there really is! The Flaming Groovies couldn't contain their annoyance, collected that night's fee in cash and did a Basil Bond (a famous French artist whose main illusion was to disappear), leaving one of their own behind.

Yep, you've guessed which one they left behind, the drummer of course.

*

These days, when you tour, you'll also have a large chunk of your fees deducted at source, in a tax known as withholding tax. If you ever get to the stage where you pay taxes in your country of origin, then the monies deducted, as withholding tax, will be deemed as a credit against all such payments. If on the other hand you don't pay taxes, it will just be lost income for you. Either way, withholding tax effects your cash flow situation drastically.

Ireland, as far as I am aware, is the only country that is prepared to give its home-grown talent a break when it comes to paying taxes. If you can prove you are of Irish descent, then they will give you 100% tax relief. But they'll only give you this break on the income you receive as a direct result of your art. That is to say, if songwriting is considered to be your art, your publishing royalties will be considered as income generated directly due through your art. On the other hand, record royalties, merchandising and touring income are all deemed to be a by-product of your art, so they'll be taxed as normal. And hopefully normal won't be quite as bad as what the taxman demanded of The Beatles, prompting George Harrison to remonstrate in 'Taxman' on *Revolver*.

Yep, the taxman's always been there and always will be, as will the various causes and charities who'll come knocking on your door once you start to raise your profile. They'll invite you, and not always politely, either to give them dosh or do a concert for them, and sometimes they'll even request both. Do as your conscience dictates, but be aware that audiences have grown cute to forking out for inflated tickets only to see their heroes do two or three songs. If you feel so strongly about a cause it might be advisable to perform a normal full concert and donate your fee or a percentage of your fee quietly to the cause.

On top of which, you will have to deal with other weird people – okay, nutters if you like – claiming that they've written your songs. This happens more than you might think and I'll refrain from giving examples here on the grounds that mud not only sticks, but also it's bloody dirty stuff as well. You did remember to mail that cassette to yourself, didn't you?

Who else will you have to deal with once you're flying high with your hard-earned profile? Let's see, okay there'll be girlfriends [or boyfriends] who'll claim that you fathered their child and who'll be claiming palimony; there'll be an ex-wife looking to increase her alimony, or an ex-boyfriend, or ex-girlfriends, claiming alimony. And even if you do pay, they'll still be willing to sell their story to one of the tabloids for a minimum of £20,000 and a max of goodness knows what, it'll all depend on your profile. And just to add insult to injury, they'll also throw in the fact that you weren't a great lover and that they were cheating on you anyway with another star, and you can read all about it tomorrow while you enjoy your fish and chips.

Even your friends will be weird with you. They'll be either nervous or overfamiliar. Sometimes they'll even be uncharacteristically shy with you. You'll be thinking to yourself, "It's me, it's the same person you used to bunk off school with!" And your friend will be thinking, "You used to be the same as me, but here you are now, transformed into an artist with thousands of people worshipping you on stage!" Your friends will not realise that even though you write songs and get up on a stage in front of thousands of people, you won't have changed.

It is their inability to accept this fact and your new status that will mess with your head.

They'll rarely behave like the good mates they once were. Of course, you'll start to make a new set of friends while touring. The same set of rules apply to us all when we're making new friends, don't they? Be careful!

On top of all the above, you'll also have to consider writing and recording your follow-up single and album. This process even has its own name, TDSAS (The Difficult Second Album Syndrome). I'm not altogether sure I subscribe to this theory, you know, that you have all your lifetime to write and record your first album and as little as 12 months to write and record your second.

If you're a songwriter, you'll have been writing away for a good few years before you get a deal. So you should have a stockpile of songs going into your second and sometimes third album. On top of which, as we've already mentioned, success begets success. Once you've been accepted commercially, once you've got over the hurdle of believing that people actually like what you do, well that in itself will be an amazing impetus for your songwriting. Try to avoid writing songs about how difficult your life has become now that you're successful. People don't want to hear that. They want and need your music as an escape from the fact that their own lives are so difficult.

The other important thing to remember here is that great song-writers don't write *singles* or *albums*. No, they write songs, which *may become* singles or songs on albums. There is a great difference and if you are very lucky they will write songs that will become hit singles or form the basis of successful albums.

★

Something happens to certain artists when they have been doing this for a period of time and have enjoyed a certain degree of success. They become what's known in the entertainment industry as "a star".

Really, Paul? Pray, tell me more.

Well, to tell you the truth, I don't really know exactly what it is that enables this metamorphosis to take place. I do feel it has a lot to do with their body of work, their ability to deal with success, their humanity, their confidence, their inner calm and their consideration and graciousness. For instance, in my humble opinion, Eric Clapton is a star and Van Morrison is not. Just to balance this out here I should point out that there are few things that Van Morrison would consider more offensive than being considered a star.

The star quality thing has nothing whatsoever to do with talent or success.

Anyway, just make sure you enjoy your success as you go; that is to say, try to enjoy your gigging.

Gigging in itself can be just a means to an end, and that's certainly fine if you are making a living from it. But if you wish for more from your performing career, then you and your agent need to also keep an eye on the bigger picture. I've never been able to figure out the saying "eye out" fully. You know, if you've got your eye *out*, you're kinda blind aren't you?

Sorry, yes . . . I'm getting back to it now . . . the big picture in live performances, right. You have to remember that if you come into town, any town, and you sell out the venue, then the promoter is certainly going to be happy. He will have made his projected profit and, at the same time, he'll have minimised his risk by playing you in a venue well within your drawing capabilities. And as I said, don't get me wrong, there is certainly nothing wrong with that, nice work if you can get it.

But, when you play to a sold-out house, you are, to a certain degree, preaching to the converted. Your fans will always be the first to rush out and buy your tickets. I think you should also spare some time to consider the people who may not have been fans at that stage, but would also like to have gone, if only to check you out. If this group of people, let's call them, "undecided", if the "undecided" are unable to see and hear you the first couple of times they try, they'll eventually give up and go off in search of other acts to be "undecided" about. So, what I'm saying is, always consider a second show, or another gig in the same catchment area or a bigger venue. Mind you, there are obviously disadvantages to bigger venues. For the kind of music I think we're discussing here, I think three nights in Hammersmith Odeon is preferable to one night at Wembley Arena. Yes, yes, I know we certainly can have the discussion about the economics and not having enough nights to spare, but when it gets down to it, in order to protect your long-term career, you need your audience to be able to see and hear you properly. Properly, in my mind, does not mean a little dot on the stage in a cavernous barn. It's all down to personal taste in the end and mine is certainly for the more performance orientated venues than the spectator type arenas.

So when you find yourself in the enviable position of being a "breaking artist", it is vitally important that you and your agent keep the choice of venues to the forefront of your collective minds. This is the key time for you to build your audience. Don't forget that once you start to peak, your audience can only go downhill from there on, so the bigger your audience is at your peak, the bigger it'll remain. Staying with farmyard similes, I think it's also known as making hay while the sun still shines.

While we're on this subject, it's also always advisable that while the basis of your concert is always going to be you and your songs, you still need to ensure that your performance, within those limits, is somewhat different every time you tour. I know there are exceptions that break the rule here but you have to ask yourself how many times would you want to see Chuck Berry, or the same movie, or the same play. Tom Waits, on the other hand, puts on a completely different show each and every time he tours, and he always sells out his concerts the first day the tickets go on sale and that's always for as many concerts as he chooses to do. He is actually one of the few artists in the world who grows in stature in his down time, that is his time off the road, a point that is continually proven by his album sales and ticket sales. In his case, his rarity value and the uniqueness of his performances definitely add to his legendary status.

Some bands obviously love life on the road and live the majority of their lives that way. They simply embrace life on the road. On the other hand, some artists fight it, some artists don't fully appreciate it, don't appreciate what was actually happening until several years later when it's too late and they're no longer in a position to perform, let alone enjoy it.

In a scene where most of the participants are preoccupied with the next gig, the next town, the next tour, you'll spot a great artist by the fact that he will be enjoying his (current) day and his (current) tour.

Okay, okay, you say, we get the picture; you feel we should enjoy it. But if we try too hard to make sure we enjoy it, aren't we totally defeating the object of enjoyment?

183

Well that's correct, to a degree. But it seems to me that if you don't go about this the right way and set your system up so you are aware of today, then not only will the time and opportunities have passed you by, but there is also a greater danger that you will lose a part of your life, of yourself, that you'll never get back again.

When you start out on this road, there is a good chance your objective will be to "make it" and to produce some great music along the way. The problem comes when you get so wrapped up in it, in achieving your goal, that you are continually driving yourself onwards and onwards, never satisfied with what you are achieving.

George Harrison talked a lot about this. About how The Beatles were so driven and then when they eventually got there, reached this mythical peak, they discovered that there was no one else there, there was nothing else for them to see or enjoy or experience. In George's case, he often claimed that he gave up his nervous system in the process.

Dire Straits, I feel, suffered from striving towards similar goals. Basically, they were a great pub band, one of the best. But they were in the right place at the right time with the right red Stratocaster guitar, and they took off. Each album bettered the sales of the last until they peaked with *Brothers In Arms*, which sold absolutely squillions. Each world tour outsold the last. But each tour they did and each album they recorded was always based on music. Then they did it one final time and maybe on that occasion their decisions were based on *making* the biggest album ever, or playing the biggest tour ever. And in that one fatal moment they won what they were after, but lost what they had, the soul of the band. They received the success they so desperately sought. But when they got there, they too found exactly the same as The Beatles had found, there was nothing there waiting for them.

And the sad thing, in both cases, was that neither group could step back again to their creative peak, the step they were on before they reached their commercial peak. By taking that final step, in a way they destroyed the magic they had.

Mark Knopfler made amends by putting together a gigging band, The Notting Hillbillies, and got out again playing the small venues, making music and having fun. George Harrison convinced some of his mates, Roy Orbison, Bob Dylan, Tom Petty, Jeff Lynne and Jim Keltner to do something similar with The Traveling Wilburys. Sadly they never had a chance to take that magic band on tour. We can only imagine how incredible that might have been.

But you know, it's not all doom and gloom, we've still got Philip

Dansette & Goggles Anonymous' career to look forward to. It'll be fun, if they want. If they're lucky, they'll have a hoot along the way, make some great music and, strangely enough, if making great music remains their priority and they've taken care to set themselves up properly, then they're sure to make a few bob along the way.

It'll certainly help if they prepare themselves for some bizarre incidents along the way, and not always from other people.

For instance, Paul? I hear you ask.

Okay, the single most frequently asked question I get is, "Do you have any troublesome clients?"

And my honest answer is, "No, I don't."

And that's a fact, a simple but true one. But they always seem to be disappointed with my answer. You know, as if I'm fibbing to protect my artists.

But you see, the question they should be asking to avoid disappointment is: "Do you have any troublesome wives, or girlfriends, of artists?"

And the answer would have to be an immediate, "Yes!"

Not many mind you, maybe even just the one in fact, and strange would have been a good word to describe her. This certain artist, who shall remain nameless – oh, come on, what do you expect for £12.95? – was appearing in Dublin's fair city where the girls *are* so pretty. The artist in question had worked up quite a sweat on stage and all of a sudden he starts to get heckled by a woman by the front apron of the stage. Anyway, this woman is generally referring to the artist's manhood, doubting his parentage and observing his weight. She was growing louder in her verbal assaults so the security did what they are meant to do – came to remove her.

The woman in question appeared to have had quite a few drinks and was, shall we say, reluctant to accompany security to sample the delights of the cold night air. So she floored a couple of the security men. A couple more members of security arrive and eventually, with the aid of headlocks and arms locks and what have you, they removed her unceremoniously from the auditorium.

You see, by her actions, security weren't to know that this woman was also the wife of the singer!

Eventually she was rescued, only to storm straight onto the stage, berate her husband and hurl a stool down into the audience, obviously aimed at one of the unfortunate security guards.

Now all this may seem very strange to you, but it's by no means the strangest bit of the tale.

The following morning, as my Ulster Fry grew cold on my plate, the singer in question grilled me about my view of what had happened on the previous evening. I recounted my tale, pretty much as above, perhaps taking care to spare his feelings. At the end of my recollection, I was greeted with: "No that's not the way it happened Paul, here's what happened . . ."

And he not only proceeded to rewrite history, but he also tried to pre-date the venue's ban on future appearances by the said artist by post-dating a ban of his own.

Denial is a malignant disease.

★

Mind you, it's not always so dour. There are lighter moments.

Okay, it's no secret by now I'm sure that artists sometimes do tend to lose it; but in another way we seem to expect nothing less from them. Elton John famously rang up his management office one day to complain about the wind blowing noisily outside his window and demanding they do something about it.

Brian Ferry allegedly tore up his passport on the eve of an American visit because he quite simply didn't like the look of his passport photograph.

There's the story of the famous folk musician who became so drunk after one of his own gigs that not only did he go into the wrong hotel room, he even went to the wrong hotel. Not surprisingly there was already someone else (a couple) in the bed, so this musician decided to make the best of a bad night, resorting to some jazz, or rock'n'roll. No, in this instance, we're not talking about the musical kind.

And there's the story that George Jones once received an advance of $100,000 from a record company. That's a lot of money these days, but in those days it was an absolute fortune. Allegedly, or so the quote goes, Mr. Jones spent the majority of the advance on cocaine; the rest he completely wasted.

Some artists are even prepared to add to their own legend. Bob Dylan loves being on the road as he proves some 150 nights a year. A few years back he did an outdoor concert near a dried-up riverbed and caught some mystery bug that had dwelt therein. For a short time before they found a cure, the rumour was circulating that he thought he was dying.

Legend has it that the star just didn't want to fade away though so he came up with the unique and career-enhancing method of taking his own life. He would get down his prize six-shooter pistols, fill them with blanks and rush into the local Wells Fargo Bank, waving and discharging the pistols towards the ceiling. Obviously the guards would have to shoot him.

The theory being that the following day he'd be prime-time news worldwide and his catalogue would tumble out of the warehouses in their millions.

*

So, that's about it. That's about it, and about the road and playing live and, as I mentioned, although the recording side of the scene has seen better days, the live side seems a great deal healthier.

I do feel that there is something stirring out there. Something is starting to bubble to the surface. It seems very much to be a song-led thing. The young artists currently sending in their demos seem to have songwriting as their priority again. This is no bad thing, as I hope you'll agree. This new scene is gathering momentum so one day, in the not too distant future, a new wave of songwriters will produce a much-needed changing of the guard. I doubt, due to the priorities of the current youth culture, that the next movement will ever be as big or as successful as the punk movement or the beat group movement or even the jazz movement, but hopefully it will set the scene for the one after that. That's all we need to keep the gigging circuit alive. At the end of the day, no matter how fashionable or hip artists or their acts might be, unless they are able to cut it up there, playing live on the stage, they are never going to last. I don't really know why, but thankfully it's just the way it works, and for that we should all be eternally grateful.

SPECIMEN CONTRACT AND RIDERS

125 Parkway, Regent's Park, London NW1 7PS
Tel: 020 7387 5090 Fax: 020 7387 8740

An Agreement Number....9905 PC........made the....9th....day of....Sept....03....

between........David Stopps....

hereinafter referred to as the "Management" of the one part.

and ....Gawks Ltd....

hereinafter referred to as the "Artiste" of the other part.

Witnesses that the management hereby engages the Artiste and Artiste accepts an

GOGGLES ANONYMOUS

engagement to   present....

appear as ....

(or in his usual entertainment) at the Dance Hall/Theatre or other venue and from the dates and for the periods and at the salary stated in the Schedule hereto.

Schedule   Date ....17th March 2004....

Venue ....Friars, Aylesbury....

Salary ....GBP 930.95....

Clauses

1.   The Artiste shall not, without the written consent of the management, appear at any public place of entertainment within a radius of....25.... miles of the venue during a period of ....4.... weeks immediately prior to and....4....weeks immediately following the engagement.

2.   The Artiste shall play for....1 x 75 minutes....see attached clauses....

3.   Salary payable by ....to ....

on/within....

Additional Clauses

4.   All signatories to this contract are advised to hold Public Liability Insurance.

5.   Any rider clauses attached form an integral part of the agreement.

Equipment arrival....Artiste arrival....

Doors open....Stage time....

Capacity ....Ticket price ....

Venue telephone number....

This Agency is not responsible for any non-fulfilment of contracts by Proprietors, Managers or Artistes, but every reasonable safeguard is assured.

Signed....

Address ....

ASGARD PROMOTIONS LTD
Directors: PAUL FENN, PAUL CHARLES VAT No: GB 340 7326 77
Registered in England No: 1048436 Registered Office as above
Member of the Agents' Association (Great Britain) & Concert Promoters Association

ASGARD PROMOTIONS LTD.
125 Parkway, LONDON, NW1 7PS
Tel: 0171-387 5090
Fax: 0171-387 8740

ADDITIONAL CLAUSE

1.   It is agreed and understood that the Management will deposit 50% of
        the total agreed Salary with ASGARD PROMOTIONS LTD CLIENTS
        ACCOUNT, number XXXXXXXX, at National Westminster Bank,
        Seven Kings Branch, Sorting Code XX-XX-XX, to arrive no later than
        17th February 2004.

It is further agreed that the balance of the Salary will be paid by cash on
night.

Signed ....

GOGGLES ANONYMOUS

This rider is intended to ensure that each engagement runs as smoothly as possible for the mutual benefit of both group and promoter. In the event that you are unable to comply with any of the following points please contact Asgard as soon as possible, preferably in writing, to avoid confusion.

ASGARD
125 Parkway
Regents Park
London
NW1 7PS
Fax: 020 7387 8740

1/ This rider forms an integral part of the agreement, thus being legal and binding to both parties. Any agreement returned with the rider unattached, unsigned or altered without prior consent from Asgard or the artist will be deemed null and void. This will be considered reason for immediate cancellation.

2/ GOGGLES ANONYMOUS to receive 100% sole top billing.

3/ The promoter agrees that the artist's crew and equipment will have access to the venue for a minimum of six hours to the public being admitted. At the same time, parking spaces for the artist's vehicles in close proximity to the stage area.

4/ A representative of the promoter, or the promoter in person, shall be present at a time specified for arrival of road crew and remain present at the venue for the duration of load in, set up, soundcheck, performance and load out.

5/ The promoter agrees to supply a minimum of 8 stage crew for load in and load out. The stage crew will work at the sole direction of the artist's crew. Also the promoter will ensure the provision of necessary ramps, ie, steps/lifts, etc. When the load in/load out is difficult the stage crew members will be increased accordingly.

6/ **Stage.** Minimum stage size: 40ft wide by 32ft deep plus PA wings. Stage to have a minimum of 30ft clearance without any obstructions.

7/ **Rigging.** We will require 4 lighting points as on the lighting plot. In some venues we will also require 2 sound points downstage of the proscenium.

8/ Proper security at all times to ensure the safety of the artist and his equipment during and after performance.

9/ The promoter agrees to provide space in a central position in the hall for the sound mixing desk, together with sufficient platforms for the desk.

Contd.

191

10/ The management agrees that no part, portion or segment of the artist's performance is to be reproduced, either audio or visually, without the express written permission of the artist.

11/ The promoter agrees that in the case of the artist being paid a percentage of the door takings then the artist's rep. must be allowed to inspect all ticket stubs (or whatever system the promoter uses in determining door takings) during and after the performance.

12/ Where fee is to be paid by deposit all payment conditions will be the essence of this contract.

13/ The promoter allows the artist the sole exclusive rights to sell shirts, records, posters, etc of the artist and to provide sufficient space for a stall to be erected. This must be at no cost to the artist and any hall fee for this facility must be paid for by the promoter.

14/ The artist requires twenty (20) tickets to be held for the sole use of the artist at each show – these tickets are to be at no cost to the artist.

Please be advised that the artist's obligation to perform is subject to illness, accident, failure of transportation, act of God, riots, strikes, labour disputes, epidemic or the order of any public authority. If the artist is prevented from performing by any of the above reasons or similar then the artist shall be under no further obligation to the management.

PLEASE BE ADVISED THIS IS A GENERIC RIDER AND ANY CLAUSES HERE MAY BE OVERRIDDEN IN THE ARTIST'S TECHNICAL RIDER OVERLEAF.

Signed .... Dated ....

GOGGLES ANONYMOUS

CATERING RIDER – as of 9/9/03

Philip Dansette's Room
1 x bottle of good quality Red Wine
6 x bottles of Heineken – must be in a fridge or well iced down
2 x litre bottles of Sparkling Water
Selection of glasses, plates, cutlery, tissues + corkscrew
Fresh Fruit bowl
Selection of cheeses: Brie, Cambozola, Stilton, Mature Cheddar.
Grapes & Crackers
Tea & Coffee making facilities
2 x towels & tissues
Bottle opener and corkscrew
1 full length mirror – essential!!!

Band Room
2 dozen cans or bottles Heineken Lager, iced down
2 dozen cans or bottles of Bulmers Cider, iced down
2 bottles of good quality Red Wine
20 x litres of Spring Water – non-sparkling
3 x litres of Sparkling Water
2 x litres of Orange Juice
2 x dozen cans of mixed Sodas (Pepsi, Sprite, etc)
lots of ice!!!
Tea & Coffee making facilities
Milk
A large fresh fruit bowl
Selection of sandwiches for 10 people
Deli tray: Ham, Cheeses, Vegetables, dips, etc
Bread, Butter, Knives, Forks, cups and real glasses, etc
Plastic glasses for Stage
Serviettes & tissues
20 towels
Bottle Opener + corkscrew
40 Half Pint plastic glasses for stage
10 hot meals after soundcheck or buy out.

ACKNOWLEDGEMENTS

Thanks are due and offered to: Dixie Kerr and Eamon Regan for the start; to Chris Charlesworth, Paul Fenn, Chris O'Donnell, Ed Bicknell, Phil Jones, Pat Savage, Christopher Runciman, John McIvor, Christina Czarnik and Steve Cheney for the foreground; to all the Asgard artists, managers and crews, long may you run; to Andrew and Cora for never ending support; AND to Catherine for all the rest.

BIBLIOGRAPHY

RECOMMENDED READING

The Art Of Record Production by Richard James Burgess (Omnibus)
Black Vinyl White Powder by Simon Napier-Bell (Ebury Press)
X Ray by Ray Davies (Viking)
The Beatles Anthology by The Beatles (Weidenfeld)
David Geffen: A Biography Of New Hollywood by Tom King
    (Hutchinson)
24 Hour Party People by Tony Wilson (4th Estate)
Long Distance Call by Richard Williams (Aurum)
Starmakers & Svengalis by Johnny Rogan (Queen Anne Press)
Fifty Years Adrift by Derek Taylor (Genesis)
Entertainment Law Review by Corrina Cree Clover★

★Vol. 23, Number 2, Loyola Law School, Los Angeles.

RECOMMENDED VIEWING

This Is Spinal Tap
Almost Famous
The Beatles Anthology

Contacts

Managers

Philip Tennent. DoubleMono Ltd, 57 St Dionis Road, London, SW6
    4UB.
    Email: doublemono@hotmail.com
Alan Robinson. ARM, PO Box 177, New Malden, Surrey, KT3 3YT.
    Email: arm4053@aol.com
Fraser Kennedy. FK Management, Dapdune Wharf, Wharf Road,
    Guildford, Surrey, GU1 4RR.
    Email: fken1035@aol.com
Bob Johnson. Southside Management, 20 Cromwell Mews, London,
    SW7 2JY.
    Email: bob@southsidemanagement.co.uk

Agents

Mick Griffiths. Asgard, 125 Parkway, Regents Park, London,
    NW1 7PS.
    T: 020 7387 5090
Emma Banks. Helter Skelter, The Plaza, 535 Kings Road, London,
    SW10 0SZ.
    T: 020 7376 8501
Martin Horne. ITB, 1st Floor, Ariel House, 74a Charlotte Street,
    London, W1T 4QS.
    T: 020 7637 6979
Steve Strange. Helter Skelter, The Plaza, 535 Kings Road, London,
    SW10 0SZ.
    T: 020 7376 8501

PROMOTERS

Pete Wilson. 3A, 4 Princeton Court, 53-55 Felsham Road, London,
SW15 1AZ.
T: 020 8789 6111
Denis Desmond. MCD, 7 Park Road, Dun Laoghaire, Co Dublin,
Ireland.
T: 00353 1 284 1747
Mark Mackie. Regular Music, 42 York Place, Edinburgh, EH1 3HU.
T: 0131 525 6700
Simon Moran. SJM, St Matthews, Liverpool Road, Manchester, M3
4NQ.
T: 0161 907 3443

PUBLISHERS

Stuart Hornall. Hornall Brothers Music, The Basement, 754 Fulham
Road, London, SW6 5SH.
T: 020 7736 7891
Peter Barnes. Plangent Visions, 27 Noel Street, London, W1V 3RD.
T: 020 7734 6892
Warner Chappell Music. The Warner Building, 28 Kensington
Church Street, London, W8 4EP.
T: 020 7938 0000

ACCOUNTANTS

Mike Donovan. E.A.I. 26a Winders Road, London, SW11 3HB.
T: 020 7978 4488
Conroy Tobin. Boundary House, 3rd Floor, 91–93 Charterhouse
Street, London, EC1M.
T: 020 7608 3633
Pat Savage. OJ Kilkenny, 6 Lansdowne Mews, London, W10 3BH.
T: 020 7792 9494

LAWYERS

Tony English. Russells, Regency House, 1-4 Warwick Street, London, W1R 6LJ.
T: 020 7439 8692

James Ware. Davenport Lyons, 1 Old Burlington Street, London, W1S 3NL.
T: 020 7468 2600

Russell Roberts. Sheridans, 14 Red Lion Square, London, WC1.
T: 020 7404 0444

RECORD COMPANIES

BMG/Conifer. Bedford House, 69-79 Fulham High Street, London, SW6 3JW.
T: 020 7384 7500

EMI/Chrysalis. 43 Brook Green, London, W6 7EF.
T: 020 7605 5000

Sanctuary Records Group Ltd. Sanctuary House, 45-53 Sinclair Road, London, W14 ONS.
T: 020 7602 6351

Universal/Island Records. 22 St Peters Square, London, W6 9NW.
T: 020 8910 3333

Virgin. Kensal House, 553/579 Harrow Road, London, W10 4RH.
T: 020 8964 6000

Warner Brothers. 28 Kensington Church Street, London, W8 4EP.
T: 020 7937 8844

PUBLICITY

Barbara Charone. MBC, Wellington Building, 28-32 Wellington Road, St Johns Wood, London, NW8 9SP.
T: 020 7483 9205

Bernard Docherty. LD Publicity, Fenton House, 55-57 Great Marlborough Street, London, W1V 1DD.
T: 020 7439 7222

Richard Wootton. Richard Wootton Publicity, The Manor House, 120 Kingston Road, London, SW19 1LY.
T: 020 8542 8101

PLUGGERS

Garth Davies. Chappel Davies, 53 Great Portland Street, London, W1W 7LG
T: 020 7299 7979

Judd Lander. Judd Lander Music PR, The Media Village, 1 Wildhill, Hertfordshire, AL9 6EB.
T: 01707 656812.

AGENTS FOR RECORD PRODUCERS

JPR Productions, PO Box 4 E & F, Westpoint, 33-34 Warple Way, London, W3 ORG.
T: 020 8749 8774

Pete Hawkins Management. 54 The Avenue, West Wickham, Kent, BR4 ODY.
T: 020 8777 9959

CATERING COMPANIES

Eat To The Beat. Studio 5, Garnet Close, Greycaine Road, Watford, Herts, WD2 4JN.
T: 01923 211 702

Eat Your Hearts Out. 108a Basement, Elgin Avenue, London, W9 2HD.
T: 020 7289 9446

PA COMPANIES

Concert Sound Ltd. Unit C, Park Avenue Industrial Estate, Park Avenue, Luton, Beds, LU3 3BP.
T: 01582 565855

Canegreen Commercial Presentations Ltd. Unit 2, 12–48 Northumberland Park, London, N17 OTX.
T: 020 8801 8133

Villa Audio Ltd. Bailey's Farm, Chatham Green, Little Waltham, Essex, CM3 3LE.
T: 01245 361694

Britannia Row Productions Ltd. 9 Osiers Road, London, SW18 1NL.
T: 020 8877 3949

BACKLINE COMPANIES

The Music Bank (Hire) Ltd. First Floor Buildings C&D, Tower Bridge
　　Business Complex, 100 Clements Road,
　　London, SE16 4EF.
　　T: 020 7252 0001
John Henrys. 16-24 Brewery Road, London, N7 9NH.
　　T: 020 7609 9181

STAGE CREW SUPPLIERS

Stage Miracles. Woodlands, School Road, Little Heath, Herts,
　　EN6 1JW.
　　T: 01707 662 500
Gallowglass Ltd. 7 Gorst Road, London, NW10 6LA.
　　T: 020 8838 0234

BUS COMPANIES

Phoenix. 29 Premier Way, Abbey Park Ind. Estate, Romsey, Hants,
　　S051 9AQ.
　　T: 01794 511152
SilverGray Carriage Co. Ltd. Unit 7, Rye Wharf, Harbour Road, East
　　Sussex, TN31 7TE
　　T: 01797 226 296
Stardes Ltd. Ashes Building, Old Lane, Holbrook Industrial Estate,
　　Halfway, Sheffield, S20 3GZ.
　　T: 0114 251 0051

TRUCK COMPANIES

Atkinson Saunders. Duckets House, Steeple Aston, Oxon, OX5 3SQ.
　　T: 01869 340247
Redburn Transfer Ltd. Redburn House, Stockingswater Lane,
　　Enfield, Middlesex, EN3 7PH.
　　T: 020 8804 0027